JOINT CURRICULUM DESIGN

Facilitating Learner Ownership and Active Participation in Secondary Classrooms

୫୦ ◆ ଓଃ

JOINT CURRICULUM DESIGN

Facilitating Learner Ownership and Active Participation in Secondary Classrooms

Patricia A. Gross
Ursinus College

LEA LAWRENCE ERLBAUM ASSOCIATES, PUBLISHERS
1997 Mahwah, New Jersey   London

Lawrence Erlbaum Associates, Inc., Publishers
10 Industrial Avenue
Mahwah, NJ 07430

Cover design by Kathryn Houghtaling

Library of Congress Cataloging-in-Publication Data

Gross, Patricia A.
    Joint curriculum design : facilitating learner owner-
ship and active participation in secondary classrooms /
Patricia A. Gross
        p. cm
    Includes bibliographical references and index.
    ISBN 0-8058-2271-2 (paper)
    1. Student participation in curriculum planning. 2.
Teacher participation in curriculum planning. 3. Education, Secondary—Curricula. I. Title.
    LB2806.15.G68 1997
    373.19—dc21   97-11807
                                              CIP

Printed in the United States of America

10 9 8 7 6 5 4 3 2

*To Michael, Steve, Nicole, Sebastian,
and the memory of my mother,
Marge M. Taylor
(9/11/09–11/8/88)*

Contents

৪০ ♦ ০১

Foreword

Maxine Greene

𝇍 ◆ ℭ

The metaphor is theater—or, more precisely, the shared activity of moving a play from script to live presentation. Images are evoked of engaged human beings who have come together to bring something new into the world. In this case, of course, they are teachers and students who have come together to shape the materials of knowledge and experience in such a fashion that new meanings will be released of those involved and for those who attend. Even as the process of play production culminates (or ought to culminate) in the transformation of ordinary reality into something new, something that opens perspectives on what might be or what ought to be, so does curriculum design as described in this book break with the taken-for-granted and the banal. By freeing learners to pose questions they may never have posed before, to articulate concerns seldom heeded before, the activities of design may alter the teaching–learning situation and infuse it with a new vitality.

In the background, of course, are the suggestive chords of what has been called *progressive* thought. In these times, and in this book, these chords announce the variations now associated with school renewal, constructivist learning, story telling, and newly conceived modes of collaboration. The old dichotomies, the old either/ors, are transcended. The writer makes one recall John Dewey's caution with regard to our tendency to think in terms of extreme opposites. In *Experience and Education* (1963), Dewey discussed the tension between the view that the mature person was obligated to impose knowledge and rules of conduct on the young and the view that education should be based on the young's personal experience. It does not follow, he said, that "the knowledge and skill of the mature person has no directive value for the experience of the immature." He went on:

> On the contrary, basing education upon personal experience may mean more multiplied and more intimate contacts between the mature and the immature than ever existed in the traditional school, and consequently more, rather than less, guidance by others. The problem then is: how these contacts can be established without violating the principle of learning through personal experience. What is indicated in the foregoing remarks is that the general principles of the new education do not of themselves solve any of the problems of the actual or practical conduct and management of progressive schools. Rather, they set new problems which have to be worked out on the basis of a new philosophy of experience (pp. 21–22).

Patricia Gross does not present herself as a philosopher; nor does she present herself as a proponent of either "extreme." She does, however, offer her readers a playing out of what a *philosophy of experience* implies when it comes to reflected-upon practice. Also, with her very original emphasis on the part to be played by students in the design of curriculum, she suggests some very interesting ways of establishing "contacts between the mature and the immature" and remaining true to the "principle of learning through personal experience." Indeed, because of her stress on the importance of collaboration, Dr. Gross expands the notion of personal experience to include participant social understandings. The learners she would enlist as codesigners with their teachers are in no sense separate, bounded individuals. They are distinctive; they do not duplicate one another; they speak in their authentic voices, once given the opportunity to do so. But, as described, they are very much members of a learning community with significantly shared experiences, values, and desires to know.

It is a dialogical involvement that seems to enrich and awaken those interested in design. Because of the encouragement of dialogue and conversation, the young people to whom we are introduced in the course of this book are released from boredom. The British philosopher Mary Warnock (1978) wrote that,

> [without the sense] of there being something which deeply absorbs our interest, human life becomes perhaps not actually futile or pointless, but experienced as if it were. It becomes, that is to say, boring. In my opinion, it

is the main purpose of education to give people the opportunity of not ever being, in this sense, bored; of not ever succumbing to a feeling of futility, or to the belief that they have come to the end of what is worth having. (p. 20)

Warnock was writing about imagination and its role in opening experience to new possibilities. Dr. Gross, as she involves her readers in the actual life of the classroom, is doing something similar. Her readers will feel very much part of the study she describes on dealing with current dissatisfactions with regard to the learning enterprise, particularly those described by young people themselves. They will find the author opening unexpected windows, vistas on what can be done concretely in bringing about changes that make a difference to the young. This can only be done by a teacher steeped in reflective practice herself, ready to risk critical approaches to the customary, prepared to open herself to the unexpected and the new. She makes the prospect of curriculum design exciting and appealing, as she invites us into her world. It is, as she herself suggests, a staged world in some particulars; but it is a world of lived life, a life of heightened consciousness when it comes to learning. There remain questions to be answered: further questions about diversity, about class, about value conflict, about subject matter. But this adds to the challenge posed by Dr. Gross. She has laid down a fertile ground for questioning, planning, and designing. Readers may be launched into new modes of action, untried modes of pedagogy. Enticing realms of meaning lie ahead.

REFERENCES

Dewey, J. (1963). *Experience and education.* New York: Collier Books.
Warnock, M. (1978). *Imagination.* Berkeley: University of California Press.

Preface

৪ ◆ ଔ

Curriculum design is integral to the process of learning, yet school boards, administrators, and textbook publishers have traditionally dictated curriculum boundaries. Recently, many teachers, parents, and communities have begun to gain greater say in curricular decision-making. However, what part do learners play? When do students get to speak for themselves?

Joint Curriculum Design assumes that learners need more central roles in curriculum concerns. This book stresses a progressive approach to secondary education in which *students and teachers negotiate* curriculum design—goals, content, methods, and assessments.

This book describes collaborative efforts between students and teachers, working together to break the isolation of the teacher and distancing of the student. Told through various voices, accounts outline key concepts and demonstrate techniques for developing classrooms that reflect joint intentions. Throughout the process, ongoing debriefings reveal self-, group, and peer evaluation by teachers and students.

A resource for reflective teaching, this book is geared toward practicing and prospective teachers who wish to alter existing patterns or develop new approaches to teaching. Suitable for courses in curriculum development or methods of teaching, this book links key components of progressive education—learner ownership, participation, and social agency—with prime concerns of educators facing the 21st century—literacy, diversity, and assessment—across the curriculum.

This book differs from other texts by (a) asking teachers to construct learning in a more inclusive manner with students, and (b) offering readers strategies they probably have not encountered in their own schooling.

The purposes of this book include three main strands: **action research** (reflective planning and practice), **critical pedagogy** (dialogue and problem-posing) and **critical literacy** (effective use of language in authentic situations). Constructivist in intent, all three strands encourage lifelong learning for teachers and students.

Joint Curriculum Design centers upon teachers and students who confronted the limits of traditional instruction, rejected the status quo, and redefined roles to make learning more meaningful. Stories derive from suburban and urban settings across a wide socio-economic range. Joint curriculum design appeals to teachers who model lifelong learning and to adolescents who, as they mature, seek relevance in their work, independence in thought, and opportunities to articulate beliefs.

Examples reveal that teachers and students displayed imagination and initiative as they increased resources for more effective learning experiences. This book invites you to join the process, to construct meaning in terms that best support mutual efforts and intentions for intellectual growth.

An extended theater metaphor frames the book to spotlight how teachers *and* students are active "players," arriving at original insights and ideas, in the spirit of inquiry and investigation, as well as through unexpected, "improvisational" moments. This book suggests strategies to build and sustain a "setting" based on "dialogue," preferably from the first class meeting, but possible at any point teachers and students wish to engage in change. (The main study in this book began mid-school year). Stories cover Grades 7 through 12 and depict the work of planning "behind the scenes," as well as "acting onstage." Anecdotal narratives exemplify and attest to the vitality of working as "ensembles."

Intentionally inductive, individual chapters serve as explorations that can stand alone, but cumulatively offer philosophies of teaching that underscore the thoughts, perceptions, and actions of various players. Each chapter examines ideas that depend on mutual trust, joint risk-taking, and shared control.

Chapter 1 introduces the background and rationales for joint curriculum design. Chapter 2 offers an overview of the elements of joint curriculum design. Highlighting the main issues, this chapter forms the "prologue" to "scenes and acts" to follow. Chapter 3 discusses how teachers choose a philosophy ("structure") supportive of classrooms designed for joint curricular planning. Veteran and student teachers share actual experiences of studying context in light of underlying beliefs, in preparation for introducing joint curriculum design.

Chapter 4 "sets the stage" by stressing classroom environmental factors ("tone or mood"). Chapter 5 examines messages and meanings implicit in actual practice ("scripts"). To illustrate how perceptions can vary, students and teachers share impressions and compare notes about classroom life. Chapter 6 explores how to establish an atmosphere of trust and joint emphases in the learning process ("interpretations")—identifying areas for improvement and planning direction for actions.

Chapter 7 investigates resources ("set design"). Reaching out to others, teachers and students multiply learning activities and experiences. Chapter 8 critiques process ("rehearsals")—noting progress, voicing concerns, raising questions, altering plans—by consensus.

Chapter 9 delves into assessment alternatives that move away from traditional tests and measurements. A range of sources record learning on a frequent and relevant basis, determining what is understood and what needs to be known. Debriefings provide feedback for reflection ("previews"). Culminating activities stress "performance" and communicate levels of understanding.

Chapter 10 anticipates the future, envisioning ongoing development of a "repertoire" of strategies for future performances ("touring company").

Joint curriculum design thrives in a reflective climate that prompts follow-up actions. Suggested topics for learning-log entries supplement questions broached throughout the text to facilitate thoughtful approaches to working "behind the scenes." Collaborative exercises challenge students to work with you and one another to explore "try-outs" to achieve a more dynamic and flexible curriculum for more effective learning.

ACKNOWLEDGMENTS

Many people inspired me to write this book. My son, Steve Mounk-hall, has been my staunchest fan and critic, actively questioning and filtering my ideas. My brother, Michael M. Taylor, has always brought wisdom and levity to balance things. Joan Dukes and Connie Lord sparked animated discussions about teaching and learning. Celia Genishi, Joe Grannis, and John Shefelbine strengthened my grasp of research. Maxine Greene stretched my imagination. Ursinus College afforded me released time; Sara Davis and Del Engstrom patiently read drafts, providing constructive comments; Paul Bashus assisted in graphics. My editor, Naomi Silverman, consistently displayed faith in my work and offered valuable insights. Joe McNicholas and Linda Henigin gave helpful advice. Reviewers Mari Koerner at Roosevelt University and Sally M. Oran at Northern Arizona University astutely assisted in framing and maintaining the coherence and integrity of my work. Special thanks to all the teachers and students with whom I have collaborated and from whom I continue to learn.

1

Playbill: Introduction

ഔ ✦ �

Using the metaphor of the theater that frames this book, consider
your role among the troupe of educators dedicated to energizing
and revitalizing secondary teaching and learning.

Collaboration works. One-person productions lack the multiple perspectives and spontaneous improvisations that human interactions
inspire. In contrast, most award-winning shows feature synergistic
casts that captivate sell-out audiences to share visions that linger
long past performances. So too, in the theater of teaching.

Collaboration empowers and liberates teachers as learners and
professionals. My experiences as secondary teacher and district
supervisor, university researcher and staff developer, college pro-
fessor and student teacher supervisor have demonstrated enduring
values of collaboration. Working with others, I have shared ideas,
taken risks, and studied results. Initiative and ingenuity have helped
us reorder priorities and reorganize physical space, social interactions, and curricular emphases for more effective teaching and
learning.

We have extended similar options to students as well. Student
voices are rarely heard and their interests often remain outside the
classroom. Deficit models label students negatively, rather than
question the system or standards of the status quo. In direct contrast,
we have afforded students active roles in decision making, which
enabled them to identify and develop strengths, while finding personal relevance in educational pursuits.

A progressive philosophy permeates my career. I stress the
necessity for learners to construct meaning, I promote the power of
literacy across the curriculum, and I highlight the significance of

1

increasingly diverse student populations. By embracing teachers and students as lifelong learners, I have created collaborations that have sparked the rewards of **joint curriculum design**.

BACKGROUND

The impetus for this book began over 25 years ago when I first entered the field as a secondary English teacher, caught in the middle of change. I observed that well-respected, veteran teachers controlled all aspects of the learning situation, whereas younger colleagues tried individualized instruction. Mentors directed me toward control mechanisms, but possibilities inherent in spontaneity intrigued me.

I recalled how I had preferred leeway in my own studies from elementary through graduate school. Being asked to direct learning for all my students felt artificial and contrary to my own experiences as a learner. Tensions between what I was doing and what I believed led me to improvise. I conferred with students and began to experiment with single sessions, then units of study. Gradually, I restructured my whole approach to teaching to reflect my underlying belief in the learner.

Outside the classroom, other events furthered my understanding of teaching and learning. The first time I was involved in writing curriculum, I worked with colleagues from other buildings in a large district. Like a summer stock company, we had 6 weeks to get acquainted, pool our strengths, and produce a writing guide for ninth-grade English teachers. We explored ideas and strategies in a lively exchange.

That experience proved rewarding for me and helpful to many teachers who found the suggested structure and sequence useful. But, administrative approaches varied across buildings and other teachers felt compelled to follow the ideas and lesson plans in strict order, page by page. This realization bothered me because I had always resisted "teacher-proof" materials that undermined self-expression and creativity. When the district employed a few faculty members to write a guide for others, they may have been well-intentioned, but too many interested parties felt silenced.

Years later, as a district supervisor of English in another large district, I introduced whole language concepts to the secondary level, in hopes of developing the voices of students and teachers. Some colleagues welcomed change and willingly embraced the premises of learning language through integrated, personalized use. But, some changes proved subtle, others only temporary. Colleagues who resisted did so not just on philosophical grounds. Instead, dedicated teachers raised concerns about content coverage, administrative demands, and parental expectations. The system stymied risk taking.

Juggling these curricular issues forced me to rethink the definitions of education, teaching, learning, and knowledge. In order to examine conflicting perspectives, I pursued a doctorate in curriculum and teaching. My studies furthered my belief in the individual learner and progressive education, which opposed the standardization of learning connected with traditional teaching.

At the university level, my collaborative research centered on the curricular issues and concerns voiced by progressives and the English departments with whom I had worked. Some clear insights emerged: (a) Greater depth rather than breadth of coverage led students to clearer understanding; (b) more opportunities for choice increased student motivation for learning; and (c) learner ownership and active participation engendered more effective learning.

Joint control of curricular decision making improved learner confidence from teachers to students, in a domino effect. We drew from each other's experiences and shared knowledge and insights to solve problems and draw conclusions. As a result, we all found pride in ourselves and our work (Gross, 1992a).

I continue to learn in the undergraduate education classes I currently teach. Students often question the freedom of choice regarding course emphasis, research topics, and due dates; they doubt the efficacy of the progressive philosophy I state up front. Some students ask me to tell them what I want; others assume they should repeat what I believe. Gradually, they realize I expect them to research issues of interest and express informed opinions (Gross, 1996).

Throughout my career, I have enjoyed working with teachers and students, to study issues and brainstorm solutions, to liberate thinking and multiply alternatives for more effective learning. Personal experiences have compelled me to share insights that have emerged from collaborations in hopes of inspiring others.

What professional collaborative efforts have you pursued? What role(s) do you expect to play over the next five years? How will you accomplish your goals?

RATIONALE

Teaching is a dynamic, ever-changing endeavor. Each success proves to be but a hint of things to come—new challenges, new discoveries. The excitement of learning led us to the teaching profession. Why not spread our enthusiasm for learning by creating an open dialogue with students to encourage interrogation of course content and methods, sustaining conversations on a daily basis?

These ideals may seem elusive for practicing and prospective teachers who often lack support or freedom to experiment. Logistics such as scheduling constraints or concerns about content coverage and standardized tests can obstruct endeavors to invigorate teaching and learning. Teachers often struggle to meet conflicting and external demands, with little support from in-service sessions that often lack clear direction or follow-up. In addition, many education courses fail to model the principles they espouse. Student teachers wrestle with theories of the latest research regarding teaching and learning, but remain unfamiliar with, and uninformed about, how to transfer these concepts into lesson planning and activities (Britzman, 1991).

Whether you are a teacher or a student teacher, you deserve better and so do your students. Countless resources lay wasted or overlooked, leaving too many individuals to operate in isolation. Joining forces stimulates higher thinking levels and creativity. Partners in learning augment possibilities for students and teachers. Powerful rewards of learning through collaboration are too valuable to be left to chance.

Need for Collaborative Curriculum Review

Curriculum constitutes the core of formal education, yet its composition and components are not always clearly stated, readily known, or regularly reviewed—especially by those most influenced and affected by it. Curriculum guidelines need to become more explicit and open to question. Curriculum changes must entail greater clarity and strive toward stronger coherence. Rather than leave curriculum decisions for district committees or textbook publishers, teachers and students deserve to confer about (a) the purposes and content of a course, (b) the methods of implementation, and (c) the means of assessment. As the individuals most closely associated with learning, teachers and students are suited to shape curriculum.

Dynamic and probing, joint curriculum design posits open examination of approaches to learning by teachers and students in relation to course content. Figure 1.1 lists key concepts behind building curriculum through ongoing dialogue. Curriculum issues and components unfold whether you read the chart vertically or horizontally.

Vertically, five verbs describe essential kinds of interaction that involve students and teachers in *joint* analysis of curriculum; five questions probe vital, interrelated issues of *curriculum*; five components imply the coherence and comprehensiveness of the collaborative *design* endeavor.

Reading the chart horizontally specifies connections: (a) Students and teachers **who communicate goals**, envision and strive toward common aims; (b) they mutually **interrogate what content** choices stimulate inquiry through individual and group interests; (c) they **negotiate methods of how** to proceed to accommodate individual needs and learning styles; (d) they **collaborate** to **sequence when** sufficient exploration and practice lead to comprehension; and (e) they devise **assessment** criteria to specify **why to inquire** into topics and determine expected outcomes.

Therefore, *joint curriculum design* is a process that may be defined as follows: **Joint curriculum design is an interactive form of**

JOINT	CURRICULUM	DESIGN
communicate	who	goals
interrogate	what	content
negotiate	how	methods
collaborate	when	sequence
inquire	why	assessment

FIG 1.1. Key concepts represented in joint curriculum design, which stresses student and teacher interaction to analyze curriculum issues and components.

planning that unites teachers and students in a joint appraisal of curricular components to negotiate goals, content, methods, and assessment throughout the various stages of planning, implementing, and debriefing.

Joint curriculum design is based on mutual trust and partnership, openness and flexibility. For example, I began applying joint curriculum design toward research writing in an average tenth-grade English class. I negotiated terms and time frames with students. We established goals and objectives, criteria for topic choices, research sources, written drafts, and final presentations. I taught research skills and served as a resource, but students also consulted with one another. Originality surfaced through self-selected collaborations and quality of work escalated. Joint curriculum design freed students to explore, confer, invent, and perform.

Considerations for Joint Endeavors

How do you and your students use your time together? What ideas and explorations excite everyone? What plans do you enact and why? What other possibilities exist?

If you invite students to critique curriculum, to join in examining what occurs in the classroom and why, students prove anxious to learn, willing to work, and eager to share new insights. Working together to uncover bases of curricular decision making, you engage in (a) recognizing common goals, (b) adjusting inconsistencies, and (c) sharpening the focus and direction of learning.

Joint curriculum design empowers students and new or experienced teachers. Stories recounted in this book affirm the innate curiosity, natural drive, and unique perspectives of students and teachers as learners. In the joint learning process, teachers and students achieved new respect for each other and for their accomplishments.

Thus, joint curriculum design moves away from traditional teaching and centers around teamwork. Instead of relying solely on the teacher, students act as valuable players with constructive suggestions to inform the process of teaching and learning.

Joint curriculum design does not dismiss the past, but recognizes the importance of balancing what proved to be effective with how to improve what didn't. Joint curriculum design invites experimentation, as individuals construct knowledge in personalized ways.

Supporting Theories

Three working theories help to develop a climate for thoughtful investigation and collaborative innovation—**action research, critical pedagogy, and critical literacy** (see Fig. 1.2).

Action research into lesson planning, content, and procedures enables teachers to study how decisions and consequences affect learning. Students become co-researchers which allows them to gain perspective, share responsibility, and contribute general insights.

Critical pedagogy frames thoughtful inquiry to effect relevant change. Joint analysis by teachers and students of course content and process isolates salient issues and identifies effective forms of investigation. Democratic classrooms train students to become critical thinkers and change agents later on in life.

Critical literacy strengthens thought and expression. Critical reading and listening facilitate ways to refine performance skills. Well-chosen written and spoken words increase clarity and cogency. Effective communication reaches a greater audience.

Thus, this book explores the potential of **changing curricular decisions into joint negotiable entities**. Joint monitoring of classroom actions and agendas enables teachers and students to appreciate the benefits of collaboration, the impact of curricular choices, and the efficacy of language for the present and future.

Examples of Collaborative Changes

This book centers on years of research with veteran and aspiring secondary-level teachers and their students. Speaking from diverse perspectives, students and teachers express initial misgivings, frequent surprises, and welcome rewards of developing curriculum collaboratively. Accounts explore transitions and represent positives and trade-offs of learning through joint curriculum design.

In numerous instances, we worked as coresearchers and shared responsibilities and insights. Deliberately nonjudgmental, we established individual parameters and welcomed differences of opinion. Breaking the isolation imposed by expert labels, we interrogated actions and perceptions. We questioned previously accepted notions, honoring some and discarding others. We attempted to first conceptualize and then actualize more congruent philosophy and

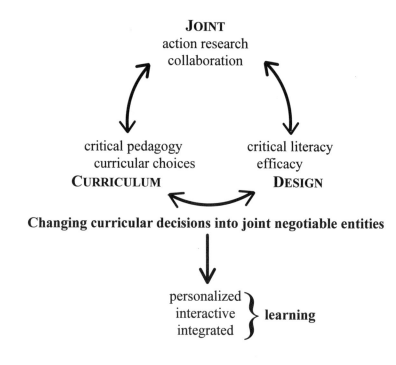

FIG. 1.2. Joint curriculum design grounds theories in the process of changing
curricular decisions into joint negotiable entities.

practice, so we could clearly identify how actions supported beliefs.
After discussing our beliefs, we surveyed students who expressed
expectations and provided frequent feedback so we could negotiate
appropriate assignments and assessments to attain joint purposes.
As a result, veteran and prospective teachers acquired new insights
and strategies that enabled students to display intellectual growth
through projects and processes, portfolios and presentations.

Scenarios differ. No one final form exists. This is not a how-to
book. Such an approach would negate the very premises underlying
our work. Instead, shared experiences leave you, the reader, to
construct learning, to adapt and adopt ideas of joint curriculum
design, in part or entirety, for your unique contexts. Narratives,
tables, questions, and reflections constitute much of the telling.
Guidelines and suggested activities encourage classroom climates
conducive to **personalized, interactive, and integrated** learning.

Joint curriculum design offers a chance to rehearse. As you read
along, the *play* and all of its elements may lead you to check out

settings and imagine direction. As you study lines, you may decide to confer with other *actors* to try out parts, videotape, and review.

The overall work does follow a logical pattern of development, but does not necessitate reading from cover to cover. Individual chapters hold certain appeal and may be read in any order that works for you. Attend to those areas that seem most promising and return to other chapters as issues arise. In the spirit of collaborative theater, choose your entrances and exits.

(Note: If you jot down ideas in a learning log as you read, you may find experimentation more meaningful. Reflectivity about what is worth doing and why or why not helps inform decisions. If you decide to write initial responses to questions posed or ideas presented, you may wish to use and date a double column entry to leave space for additional comments at a later time.)

Far from definitive, this book challenges you to write a sequel. As joint curriculum design evolves, so do insights and innovations, energizing the learning process for teachers and students. If you have ever worked in theatrical productions, whether as an elementary school child or an adult, you know that things rarely go as planned. **There is no one way, no perfect performance**. The unexpected and the unpredictable will breathe new life into your work.

Joint curriculum design is not a fad, nor a doctrine, but a refreshing philosophy based in collaboration among students and teachers. Joint curriculum design establishes a working theater from which original and memorable performances can spring.

2

Entering the Theater:
New Beginnings

℘ ◆ ℈

As you push aside the curtain to envision the types of plays you would like to create on the stage of your classroom, invite students to help bring those images to life.

A bare stage, stripped of all props, screens, and equipment, awaits transformation. Memories of past performances and productions linger, but the prospect for brand new beginnings opens the way for invention. Though formal theater upholds past precedents, adhering to original scripts and stagings, alternative or working theater studies the past to invent the future.

Willingness to experiment enlivens schooling, as it does the world of theater. Alternatives to traditional approaches broaden perspective. Advances that have transformed stages into docudramas or musicals have elevated theater-going. *Porgy and Bess, West Side Story*, and *Angels in America* enriched our lives and spirits. Controversial social issues found vivid expression through the lively arts. Similarly, innovation has transformed ordinary classrooms into active spheres of learning, nurturing individual talents and heightening social awareness.

Throughout the 20th century, educators have set the stage for students to play a more active part in their own education and the improvement of society. Dewey (1899) highlighted students' needs and championed "learning by doing" and social consciousness. Kilpatrick (1925) stressed student-generated projects linked to the community. Greene (1978, 1988, 1995) advocated the arts and imagination as avenues for richer personal lives and more pervasive social justice. Sizer (1985) fought the "conspiracy of the least" to inspire students and teachers to restructure schools and pursue interdisciplinary learning. Meier (1995b) developed intellectual habits of mind through teacher research, parent outreach, and student empowerment in schools within schools. All of these educators recognized the power of collaboration to transform schooling at first and society later on.

Inspired by these innovators and determined to make a difference, I have dedicated my career to creating opportunities for learners to take the lead, to star in their own shows. Enthusiastic responses and positive feedback have caused others to inquire about how to take similar steps to enliven the process of learning.

FRAMEWORKS FOR CHANGE

In one instance, two friends and former colleagues, Lorraine and Sarah (assumed names), sought my assistance in revitalizing teaching. They bristled under systemic restraints and wanted to get themselves and students out from under, to rejuvenate themselves and to better prepare students for thoughtful living. Lack of congruence between the type of classes they envisioned and daily routines propelled them to take action.

Lorraine explained in a journal entry:

I still enjoy teaching because of THE KIDS—they're always changing, challenging, pushing me to do more and different activities.

They make me feel young, alive, still vital, a part of the flow of life.

I feel I have something to give them, too—experience, understanding, knowledge, concern, patience.

I especially feel good when I see them involved in the teaching–learning process. It seems far too long, I've been doing the learning, relearning in the classroom and they observe me—LEARNING. I want to get them into the magic circle.

Sarah also provided insights into her incentives:

I hope to learn a way to make my job easier and have the students learn even more. I hope to involve the ones I'm not reaching now so they, too, can have the satisfaction of learning and feeling competent ...

I am also interested in trying new theories because it is exciting professionally and intellectually. It keeps me fresh and energized and there is always the chance that it will work better!

Well-respected by school and community members, both Lorraine and Sarah had always been active in the large suburban district where they have taught all levels and grades of English (7 through 12), as well as evening college preparation courses. They have advised extracurricular activities and served on various committees, in addition to writing curriculum guides in the summer.

Lorraine, a mother of four grown sons, taught for years before their arrival, then returned to teaching once they reached school age. Her experience in rural and suburban schools, at different periods of time, broadened her perspective of teaching and learning.

Sarah, a single parent of two teenage sons, taught for over 20 years in the same school where she had completed her student teaching. The chairperson had been the only supervisor who had evaluated her work until the year of the study when district policy changed.

I had taught in the same district with them for 10 years. They wanted to know what strategies I had used during my tenure there when I designed and implemented a program for talented and gifted students and then transferred those methods to the regular classroom. They wanted to learn new ideas from my subsequent supervisory experiences and doctoral studies. In answer to their request, I described joint curriculum design and the importance of reflective teaching, learner choice, active learning, ongoing assessment, and debriefing.

I offered to become a coresearcher in their classrooms to introduce them and their students to joint curriculum design. They welcomed the prospect of working together on-site and the novelty of the nonjudgmental and open-ended nature of the plan. After years of close, critical supervision, they found it refreshing to have the chance to take risks without recrimination. However, they shifted uneasily between enthusiasm for change and doubt about implementation.

Sarah compared our plan with past experiences:

The concern I have is that I don't want another pie-in-the-sky experience like individualized instruction where I have 10 times more work to do and the students waste time in the classroom not doing work unless the teacher's standing with their group. I want the students to learn and I hope this will increase learning.

That is what is bothering me—fear of not having learning increase and having a lot more work, fear of having no support at school like individualized instruction. I felt I was operating in a vacuum then as I was the only one. Come to think of it—I'm not alone here. Lorraine is doing it, too, and we have Pat for advice and support.

Their candor helped to reinforce the mutual trust and autonomy needed for collaboration. Change can be disconcerting, even when sought. Feelings of inadequancy or insecurity can undermine the best intentions of the most qualified people. They questioned how much they would have to relinquish the expert role and worried about the unknown consequences of the changes they would try. They wondered how much students would benefit.

Years of successful experiences of working with teachers and students to implement joint curriculum design had demonstrated to me that teachers found renewed interest in teaching, professional growth, and increased confidence in students. Students gained knowledge, self-esteem, and strategies for learning.

Assurances stem from the fact that joint curriculum design does not operate from a traditional lock-step approach, because every class proves unique. After analyzing regular teaching practice, the teacher confers with each class of students to consider whether to follow, adapt, or reject any suggestions that arise. Together they decide what to pursue or discontinue.

I functioned as consultant, facilitator, and guide, offering options that teachers eventually extended to students. Hands-on learning engendered valuable insights that crossed cognitive, affective, and social domains. Teachers reconsidered standard practice once they experienced the feelings and features of the types of learning possible when learners negotiate how to proceed and jointly evaluate the effects of their efforts.

My enthusiasm had caused Lorraine and Sarah to request collaboration and reassured them to some extent, but only personal experiences convinced them.

Logistical Considerations

Supportive Feedback. Joint curriculum design does not require the presence of an observer in the room, but works well when a circle of participants can provide feedback. Students and parents can become prime sources, but so can supportive colleagues. **With**

whom can you reciprocate in observing one another's classes—through videotape, if not in person? Teaching the same discipline is not as important as having confidence in each other to provide honest and constructive feedback.

Debriefing Time.   Blocks of time dedicated to debriefing allow for productive discussions of plans, lessons, and changes. For example, Lorraine and Sarah collaborated all week long. During the 3 days a week when I was present, we conferenced during lunch or preparation times for immediate feedback. For a more relaxed and fruitful exchange, we met every Friday afternoon at my home, to discuss experiences of the past week and plans for the next. We then focused on the progress of the entire project. The three of us cherished these uninterrupted after-school hours of venting, rejoicing, and regrouping.

Written Records.   Written reactions before, during, and after stages of experimentation created valuable working documents for constructive change and comparisons over time. I took copious notes in a variety of forms (see chapter 5). Lorraine and Sarah maintained learning logs throughout the study to record impressions. Even though writing these logs added yet another layer of work, they found the benefits supported regular, if not daily, entries. Students wrote reactions regarding whether or not they learned more effectively. We reviewed these records on an ongoing basis, sharing insights and posing strategies for adjustments.

Reflective Practice.   The chance to study teaching together inspired new ideas and reaffirmed beliefs. As we examined strategies, reactions, and outcomes, we applied reflective practice (Schon, 1987, 1990) that we **experienced collaboratively and extended to students**.

Reflective practice is also integral to teacher training. I teach graduate or undergraduate students who seek certification in any one of 13 secondary school subject areas and student teach in suburban or small urban districts. One student teacher expressed her frustration with comments from her cooperating teacher:

> When I had told her I was expected to try out new methods, she told me that she understood if I needed to please my supervisor and indicated that she

would *allow me the room* to do so. Her attitude is that none of these methods are new, she has tried them all and they haven't worked. She claims she is open to trying new methods again, but only if someone can "prove it to her" that they work better than the status quo way she is doing things ...

I want to try new things myself, and not just to please my superviser. It's really hard for me to stand up there and teach by trying out these methods, not knowing how well they will work myself, when I know she is sitting in the back of the room convinced that I am wasting my time.

Pressures placed on this student teacher parallel friction found in many schools, where desire for change collides with entrenched attitudes. Change disturbs people who prefer familiar patterns of behavior, but reflective practice induces change for the better.

If teachers don't model and pursue lifelong learning, who will? Do we have the right to ask students to engage in activities we ourselves avoid?

Curricular Concerns

Fortunately, support continues to grow for expanding methods of teaching to produce more effective learning. The scope of the theater of education stretches beyond traditional teaching as studies in psychology, sociology, and linguistics have challenged educators. Concepts like cooperative learning (Johnson & Johnson, 1991; Kagan, 1988; Slavin et al., 1985) and multiple intelligences (Gardner, 1991; Sternberg, 1990) prompt players to interact through a variety of forms. Issues of gender, race, and class urge teachers and students to rethink roles, pose questions, take risks, ascertain multiple meanings, work together.

Paradigm Shift.   The shift away from traditional teaching is more pronounced than ever. Teachers no longer cling to one method of acting or a single script. The lecture method and literary canons vie with a range of strategies and a wealth of resources for center stage. Views of knowledge have broadened and multiplied. Amid the seeming chaos of changes, curriculum guidelines provide structure.

Curriculum Purposes.   The broad base of curriculum defies any simple definition, but for our purposes, **curriculum encompasses the who, what, how, when, and why of educational pursuits** (see Fig. 1.1). Curriculum serves two functions: offering knowledge to individuals and socializing them for citizenry. The many facets of curriculum include plans, experiences, systems of learning, fields of study, and areas of subject matter (Ornstein & Hunkins, 1988). Controversial issues occur regularly and constituencies exert pressures. Decisions regarding curriculum shape and reflect district, building, and department cultures. Akin to nested Russian dolls, a classroom culture resides within these larger cultural communities (see Fig 2.1).

Within this system, classroom curriculum may be set by a teacher, but the actualized curriculum, or what each student actually learns, holds lasting value. That real learning depends on each learner's level of knowledge and compliance. Thus, curriculum development is the most crucial dimension of teaching and learning.

Definition of Knowledge. **What constitutes knowledge? What unstated assumptions underlie classroom purposes, content, and methods? How well do actions produce desired effects?** Answers to these curriculum questions are neither simple nor permanent. Prevailing standards of the status quo in society and schooling warrant scrutiny. Eurocentric traditions have privileged certain facts and people, excluding whole races, classes, and seg-

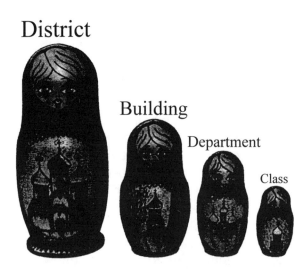

FIG. 2.1. Levels of culture that impact curriculum development.

ments of society from full participation in learning or living. Often unconsciously, these thought patterns and modes of operation dominate classrooms and the whole educational enterprise. The formative years spent in school are too precious to leave influences, practices, and perspectives unexamined. Curriculum requires deliberate, dedicated interrogation on a regular basis.

Lorraine and Sarah considered these questions throughout our project. For most of their careers, they had taught a primarily White, middle-class population whom they tried to expose to broader perspectives. A recent influx of students from various parts of the world increased the necessity for honoring diverse histories and viewpoints. Besides matters of content, demographic changes also called into question methods of providing and eliciting information.

As Banks (1994) and Nieto (1996) argued, dealing with diversity does not mean one-day or one-month recognition of the accomplishments of a group, but calls for active learning on the part of teachers and students to understand various cultures and develop responsiveness to differences. Diversity infuses life and must infuse the curriculum.

Hidden Curriculum. Curriculum choices highlight some matters and omit others. Decisions privilege some facts and beliefs over others. Lessons are learned through form and content.

Conflicting realities prompted Lorraine to write:

> School life should prepare students for the adult world. A cooperative learning approach is imperative today because students have been removed from the structure previous generations have had—at home, in church, with peers. Yet we expect them to function in a traditional school setting that forbids socialization and accountability for each other.

She worried that the lack of social structures fragmented the lives of many students, yet she realized imposed school structures did not provide stability. Arbitrary school rules or procedures complicated student understanding of individual responsibility and group cohesiveness.

School systems must support curriculum purposes of developing individual accountability and socializing students toward building coalitions. Practices that curtail individual thinking and choice leave students powerless or rebellious in attempts at self-expression. Without opportunities to work with others to achieve common goals, students feel isolated and disconnected. Mixed messages leave students confused and unprepared for lifelong personal and professional responsibilities and relationships that depend on cooperation for success.

Theater Metaphor

The metaphor of theater prompts some answers to these concerns. Theater embraces individual efforts as groups work toward production. A playwright provides content; the director communicates a vision; actors and stagehands contribute to the unfolding and shaping of that vision. A dynamic tension pushes each player to perform at his or her best. Similarly, school has the potential for offering students active roles and interdependence.

Each classroom is a stage upon which players interact to construct and derive meaning. Teachers may direct actions, setting a mood or tone. Classes of characters then react to situations built around the synergy of set design, storylines, and dialogue. Teachers and students produce daily performances, assessed by themselves and audiences of parents and administrators, as well as outside critics in future employment and advanced study.

However, the richness of teaching as theater is rarely realized. Regular routines and stereotypical roles result in rote performances by seeming caricatures, repeating well-worn lines. Depth and breadth of action and character often remain unexplored. With more voice and incentive, students could give inspired performances.

Unlike formal theater that adheres to age-old scripts and stagings, joint curriculum design resembles a form of working theater that employs ongoing dialogue to focus players to share visions. By strengthening individual and group voices, joint curriculum design raises the level of critical thinking, delves into motivations, acknowledges divergent thinking. As a result, differences of opinion and disequilibrium of ideas become rich material for reflection and dialogue. As common purposes become more explicit and better articulated, concerted actions ensue.

Casting Roles.   Think back to your own schooling. **What roles did you play in the classes you remember most fondly? How did your favorite teachers act? What activities do you still recall?**

Through the years, my students inevitably name teachers who inspired curiosity and creativity, and recall well-structured projects that entailed working with others and publicly displaying knowledge.

Next, consider your classroom as a stage that reflects your personality, interests, and intentions. In the role of director, you set mood and tone, indicating your attitudes and perceptions about *who* and *what* you teach, *how* and *when* you proceed, and the overarching *why* behind your plan.

Now, consider the dozens of actors who share that space on a regular basis over a course of time. Each presence makes a difference, but to what extent?

In what ways do students get involved? Do they comprise the audience or perform on stage? Do students only play bit parts or do they star in leading roles?

Stage directions guide actions, scenes, and script. If you read between the lines of your plan book, you'll find the patterns of content, delivery, and relationships that exist. Dewey (1899) characterized passive learning, uniform curriculum, and single methods as "old education" a century ago. Students need prominent parts to discover ideas, cooperate with others, and demonstrate knowledge actively and uniquely.

Rating Performance. **How do you frame curriculum emphases and omissions, methods of presentation and assessment, and connections with student prior learning and future goals?**

Teaching, like theater, faces ratings and criticism. Modes and methods grow stale, long-standing practices lose impact and relevancy (Britzman, 1991; Reagan, Fox, & Bleich, 1994). Teachers who follow the same old routines fail to capture minds and imaginations. Rather than repeat the past, fashion the future.

Ongoing assessment through a variety of measures assures learners of progress. Individual, peer, and teacher forms of evaluation provide feedback about accomplishments and areas for improvement. Ratings based on clear criteria provide added incentive to achieve.

Benefits of Student–Teacher Collaboration

With thoughtful exchange of ideas, teachers and students can develop learning experiences that involve interdisciplinary projects and group investigations. Possibilities abound if time and space, attitudes and perceptions (a) allow for experimentation, (b) avoid prescription, and (c) encourage learning from what appear at first to be mistakes.

What innovations have you experienced as a student or tried as a teacher? What seemed successful? What was learned from apparent mistakes?

Joint curriculum design engenders creative teaching and learning. No longer left to the way things have always been, this approach invites imaginative changes for the sake of improving classroom climate and student involvement—education for its own sake.

Joint curriculum design views the logic and use of curriculum in its entirety, endeavoring to attain greater clarity and coherence. What is not clear is a specific starting point. Because each context varies, no single answer exists. False starts will happen and questionable ideas will arise, but expecting the unexpected has always been inherent in teaching. Schedules and plans are only guidelines, not guarantees. Joint curriculum design releases teachers from the burden of trying to control unpredictability by uniting them with students to find ways to capitalize on serendipity.

Traditionally, the stage has always been set by the teacher who took charge of every detail, from decorating the classroom to developing final exams. In preparation for such a job description, education courses stressed the role of teacher as decision-maker, often causing student teachers to reel under the weight of having to make so many decisions. Many tenured teachers eventually reduced the number of decisions by ignoring certain dimensions of the job—using lesson plans year after year regardless of changes in student populations or administering the same tests repeatedly, invalidating their worth.

Joint curriculum design asks why any one person would have to answer for so many. Higher expectations of learners produce greater strides toward accomplishment. If given voice, students add resources, pose problems, design projects, evaluate performance. Joint curriculum design not only builds on strengths of the teacher, but also challenges students to be concerned and accountable.

Joint curriculum design assumes that ownership empowers students to channel their energies for shaping thoughts and constructing meaning, for more personalized and permanent learning.

The philosophy behind joint curriculum design does not provide a neat and tidy prescription. To the contrary, it acknowledges that learning, like life, is often fuzzy and messy. Rather than tighten logistics to give the appearance of control, joint curriculum design does the opposite, loosening curricular components to excite curiosity and expand learning. Joint curriculum design welcomes creativity, freedom of imagination, and use of personal background knowledge.

The following checklist of considerations offers many points of entry. The order of chapters suggests one sequence among many by which to analyze your classroom. Follow the order if it appeals to you; pick and choose if it doesn't. Scan the whole text to decide where to begin to mold and shape components according to the final performances you and your students seek.

ELEMENTS OF JOINT CURRICULUM DESIGN

Joint curriculum design delves into and derives from the following considerations, pictured in Fig. 2.2. The elements essential to joint curriculum design are never linear, nor static. Like parts of a mobile, they move freely in unpredictable paths, yet never move too far from one another. They remain connected by an overall desire to maintain and sustain a high degree of collaboration among students and teachers.

Philosophies of Education (the Focus of Chapter 3)

Throughout this century, progressive educators have held opposing views from traditionalists. This dualistic lens has filtered educational reform efforts, categorizing issues and trends on one or the other end of a pendulum. Joint curriculum design stems from a nondualistic view of learning that allows greater freedom of movement.

What traditional ideas of education are effective? What progressive ideas hold appeal? Does following only one paradigm limit teaching and learning?

Environments of Learning (the Focus of Chapter 4)

Physical arrangements send cues that cause emotional and psychological reactions by those present. Plans for the time and people engaged in a space indicate expectations. Joint curriculum design involves analyses of classroom climate influences on actions and reactions.

How will the setting be utilized? What purposes have been determined and by whom? What plans direct efforts toward achieving those purposes?

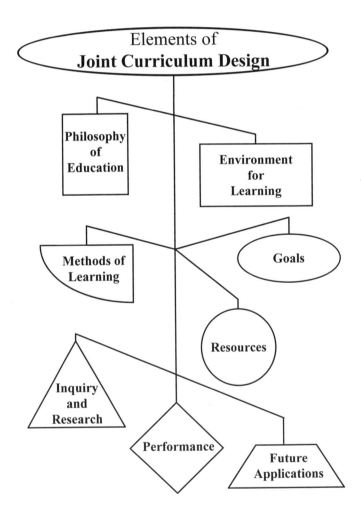

FIG. 2.2. Interplay of elements in the process of joint curriculum design.

Methods of Learning (the Focus of Chapter 5)

No two people acquire or retain information in the same manner or to the same extent. Each learner filters new knowledge through previously developed lenses and attaches new meanings to personally developed schemas. Dialoguing with students reveals preferred styles of learning.

How much do approaches to teaching vary? In what ways are learner differences met? How often are students polled to determine how they learn best?

Goals (the Focus of Chapter 6)

Goals establish course content. They prioritize topics, establish emphases, and direct learning toward specific achievements and outcomes. They define purpose and focus actions.

Who selects goals? How often are course goals reviewed or refined? Do students provide input?

Resources (the Focus of Chapter 7)

The relationship between goals and resources can be restricting. Rather than limit goals due to resources that always seem scarce, expand horizons by involving people and materials within a broader radius, revisioning and recycling resources for optimum use.

How are resources defined? Do learners form a community? How far does the circle of learners extend?

Inquiry and Research (the Focus of Chapter 8)

Investigating ideas and how they relate is downright exhilarating. From infancy, we explore unique views of the world around us in attempts to make sense of it all. Allowing students to bring this real-life tendency into active use in the classroom gives personal and relevant meaning to academic pursuits.

In what ways do students pose problems and probe issues that concern them? How much experience do students have with the realities of research? Do they refine research questions as they uncover information?

Performances (the Focus of Chapter 9)

Learners involved in active pursuit of knowledge do not wait for a final examination to express learning. As students investigate topics and test hypotheses, they continually manipulate data and draw tentative conclusions. Working portfolios and works in progress attest to productivity.

How much opportunity are students afforded to self-report or peer-evaluate throughout the learning process? Do students usually exhibit knowledge only on paper? What types of student presentations do you encourage? How often do students get to share and defend findings?

Future Applications (the Focus of Chapter 10)

Joint curriculum design prepares learners for lifelong pursuit of knowledge. Habits of curiosity, inquiry, reflectiveness, and collaboration spur learners to become informed citizens and agents of constructive change.

What habits of mind and mastery of learning have prepared learners for full, thoughtful lives? How have students demonstrated constructive impulses and social instincts?

SUMMARY

This chapter provided an overview of the rationale behind joint curriculum design and outlined elements that comprise implementation. New scenes and scripts of teaching and learning await your invention. **The suggestions that follow offer ideas for learning log entries that may help focus your thoughts before gleaning student responses. Collaborative exercises create ways of collecting student opinions for review and discussion.**

Behind-the-Scenes Mental Preparation: Suggestions for Learning Log Entries

1. Review your schedule of classes and describe the differences in course content and class chemistry. Chart the characteristics and

measure them against the traits you feel you need to have in the class(es) you would like to select for experimentation.

2. Define teaching, learning, knowledge, and education. As you attempt to draw distinctions, identify past learning situations that have influenced your definitions of these terms. Highlight key words that reveal assumptions. Ask a colleague for feedback to gain perspective.

3. Identify the element(s) of joint curriculum design most appealing to you. For each element, list different strategies you have tried or would like to explore. Outline specific actions you wish to take to develop conscious and broader attention to each element.

On-Stage Tryouts:
Collaborative Exercises to Determine
Where to Start—All or Some May Fit Your Context

1. Ask students to recall plays, movies, or videos they have enjoyed or been involved in producing. Ask them to apply the theater metaphor to school and describe the classes they have enjoyed, giving specific reasons to support choices. Request suggestions on how to enliven class to increase learning.

2. Engage students in differentiating among the terms *education* and *knowledge*. In the course of developing distinctions, help students identify the hidden assumptions in the words they choose. Discuss the consequences of those assumptions in terms of motivation and responsibility for learning.

3. Define joint curriculum design and ask students to write a paragraph or page response. Group them to discuss initial reactions and request that each group map out concerns and attractions to share with the class on large poster paper. Tape these reports to the classroom walls for future reference.

4. List the elements that comprise reorganizing education according to joint curriculum design. Ask students to define the terms individually on paper. Pair students to compare and refine definitions. Ask them to prioritize the elements from the most important to the least. Discuss with the entire class which element(s) they would like to work with first and determine whether sequencing would facilitate change.

3

Philosophies of Acting: Belief System

Behind the scenes, structures frame performances. The philosophy behind joint curriculum design espouses active learning by students and teachers.

A philosophy grows out of past experiences and forms the bases for future actions, yet few teachers ever articulate, much less review, assumptions guiding their work. If you have tried to define teaching and learning, education and knowledge, you have begun to write out the philosophy that directs your actions and those of your students on the educational stage.

PHILOSOPHICAL FOUNDATIONS

The rich history of educational foundations in the United States has tended to divide into two sides. The existence of traditional teaching prompted progressive movements, in opposition. As a result, dualistic views created clear-cut extremes, each rooted in different views of knowledge and of the relationship of teachers and learners to that knowledge (Cuban, 1990). The following definitions show how each orientation casts characters and determines roles in the learning process.

Traditional teaching transmits highly structured basic subject matter, providing efficient means for covering substantial content (Rosenshine & Stevens, 1986). A traditional setting requires characters to uphold specific roles. Teachers act as experts in specific disciplines; students function as passive receptors of predetermined instruction. The action, like formal theater, depends on set scripts.

On the other hand, **progressive teaching promotes experiential learning, integrates skills and knowledge, and cultivates individuality within social responsibility** (Dewey, 1948). A progressive setting prompts cooperative learning and an interchange of roles. Teachers share expertise, but also construct knowledge with students in a community of learners that welcomes interdisciplinary learning. More like a working theater, learners pursue individual interests or group activities and demonstrate knowledge in a variety of performances.

Thus, traditional teaching establishes foundations of knowledge and honors the past, whereas progressivism invites individual inquiry and construction of knowledge. Each distinct view of knowledge and its acquisition shapes how players think, move, and perform.

Comparison of Philosophical Approaches

Figure 3.1 deliberately presents a two-column format to suggest the duality that has split education and has led to metaphors that troped educational reform as a cycle or pendulum (Cuban, 1990)—restricted in movement. Another option exists: With an emphasis on collaboration to highlight learner talents and group strengths, **joint curriculum design** suggests a theater metaphor.

Where would you place teaching on this chart? Do you edge toward one side? Do your beliefs and actions match?

The principal focus of traditional teaching is the content and form of a specific discipline, whereas progressives value process and inquiry, often of an interdisciplinary nature. Joint curriculum design draws from both concepts, by delving into substance through a range of teacher–student negotiated topics, emphases, and activities across disciplines.

The setting for traditional teaching is fixed and competitive, usually isolating students from one another and pitting them against each other for standardized tasks at a uniform pace. The setting for progressive thinking personalizes learning. Fluid and flexible, space and time in joint curriculum design derive from individual investigations, as well as collaborative endeavors that encourage learners to join forces to achieve multiple goals.

TRADITIONAL		PROGRESSIVE
CONTENT FORM	**FOCUS**	PROCESS INQUIRY
FIXED COMPETITIVE	**SETTING**	FLEXIBLE COLLABORATIVE
TEACHER AUTHORITY STUDENTS PASSIVE	**ROLES**	COMMUNITY
ISOLATED DRILLED	**SKILLS**	INTEGRATED PERSONALIZED
TEACHER- DETERMINED	**GOALS**	NEGOTIATED
STANDARDIZED	**TASKS**	INDIVIDUALIZED
UNIFORM	**PACE**	INDIVIDUAL / GROUP
TEACHER- CENTERED	**APPROACH**	LEARNER- CENTERED
LINEAR SEQUENTIAL LEARNING	**ASSUMPTION**	UNIQUE RECURSIVE LEARNING

FIG. 3.1. Distinctions between traditional and progressive curriculum components.

Traditionally, skills have been taught to whole classes through drills of repetitive worksheets, whereas progressives integrate skills as need arises in authentic applications. Joint curriculum design seeks compromise, often resulting in group-selected ways to apply skills.

The principal approach of traditional learning is direct teaching. In contrast, progressivism stresses learning by doing. Joint curriculum design combines these approaches because the teacher shares knowledge, but in a community of active learners who are encouraged to broach topics and pursue opposing or novel ideas.

The principal assumption of traditional teaching is that learning is linear and sequential. Characterizing some learning in this way makes sense, to a larger extent in some disciplines than others. But, in every field, other learning also occurs. Therefore, the principal assumption of joint curriculum design acknowledges linear, sequential learning as well as individual, recursive learning. Not bowing to either end of the spectrum, joint curriculum design operates in a more open fashion than dualistic premises allow.

Distinctive Features of Joint Curriculum Design

- Joint curriculum design promotes a learning partnership, experiential inquiry, and critical thinking.
- Joint curriculum design values teacher expertise. However, teachers impart information sparingly to pique students to verify or question information to draw and substantiate their own conclusions.
- Joint curriculum design honors disciplinary principles and foundational information. However, joint curriculum design questions, rather than accepts, the status quo. Students probe into disciplinary form and content, seek interdisciplinary connections, and refine research questions.
- Joint curriculum design gives students options regarding topic choice and method of inquiry. A class may decide to investigate controversial issues and hold debates. A mini-lesson about key issues or debate format may result in straight lecture by the teacher, but the thrust of the unit would be student generated.
- Joint curriculum design embraces learners, content, method, sequencing, and assessment. Students gain voice in all curricular components because each element is interdependent in the learning process. With emphasis on lifelong learning, joint curriculum design challenges teachers and students to sift through content, pose new problems, and devise new avenues of investigation.

UNDERLYING MOTIVATIONS

Underlying motivations of teachers and students impact teaching and learning, yet outward expression and comparison of attitudes and beliefs rarely exist. A serious lack of communication complicates daily and long-term progress. Joint curriculum design calls for breaking silence. As teachers and students consult, less time and energy are spent distracting one another from purposeful educational goals.

Joint curriculum design presents a comprehensive approach to actualizing a teaching–learning partnership. To prepare for joint

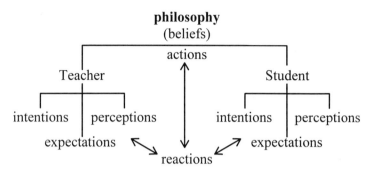

FIG. 3.2. Interplay of philosophical influences.

decision-making with students, guidelines below suggest how to chart **actions** and articulate **intentions, perceptions,** and **expectations,** then solicit student impressions. From this exchange, **reactions** can be analyzed to establish mutual ownership in the learning process. Figure 3.2 illustrates these five aspects.

Actions—Approaches to Learning

Joint curriculum design combines individual endeavors with group goals through an interplay of roles. As a prerequisite to recognizing how roles develop in the classroom, teachers examine actions to identify (a) how beliefs impact decisions, (b) whether goals match implementation, and (c) if student needs are being met.

Choices and purposes that only reflect the teacher's agenda do not necessarily satisfy student needs. Rather than operate in a vacuum, teachers can verbalize beliefs, offer options, and consult with students to plan for more meaningful activities.

Rather than expect the same response from each group or class, joint curriculum design stresses individualization. Teaching and learning situations offer a variety of roles. At first, assigning roles may familiarize students with the types available, but as a rule, roles of **players, directors, prompters, audience,** and **critics** rotate. Each participant adopts one of these roles for a time, then performs a different part, depending on the topic, group needs, and individual abilities.

Players communicate ideas and interact to make some sense out of new information; **directors** influence how players act; **prompters** inquire into action, seek clarification, and challenge choices; **audi-**

FIG. 3.3. Spiral action of learners' roles.

ences listen and respond, providing immediate verbal and nonverbal feedback to ideas; **critics** analyze action over time, causing players to debrief to ascertain how closely intentions and actions match.

This spiral action, depicted in Fig. 3.3, reinforces the interdependence that underscores joint curriculum design. Each of these roles is integral to the production of knowledge, not through artificial division among learners, but through natural expression of thoughts and understandings. Learners increase strategies for learning as they rotate through roles.

What role(s) do you play? What role(s) do students play? What beliefs underscore these roles?

Intentions—Learner Hopes and Dreams

In collaborations to implement joint curriculum design, colleagues have surprised me by countering my suggestions with words like, "Can I do that?" They doubt methods they have not experienced. Years of traditional education as students, coupled with traditional limits on teaching, have narrowed visions. Scientific, rational approaches to learning have dominated, precluding the intuitive (Noddings, 1995), imaginative (Greene, 1995) and nurturing (Grumet, 1988) dimensions of learning. If the affective domain is reintroduced, learning increases as individual intentions enter the scene.

Intentions denote determination to achieve some goal. Teachers and students enter the classroom at different points. District guidelines and daily lesson plans mark places on the stage from which players perform, but the outcomes may not achieve desired effects if intentions of teachers and students as learners are overlooked.

Teachers as Learners. Teachers learn every day, but external influences can thwart the best talents and intentions. Here, Lorraine and Sarah share how they entered teaching to spread a love of learning. Typical of many educators in their time, they found that laudable intentions became subordinated to district, building, or department mandates:

Lorraine:

I did my student teaching in [name omitted] High School, under a woman whom I felt was more than a master teacher. She did not teach subject matter; she taught worldly-wise boys who were training for a vocation and could care less about academics (and especially English—ugh!). Without exception, they loved her. Macbeth was presented as a Jimmy Hoffa, power-crazed individual. *Hiroshima* was a story of what atomic warfare could do to any country. Poetry was music—"Poetry in Motion," a popular rock and roll song of the time, was her rationale for teaching Wordsworth and Keats. Needless to say, I wanted to be just like her.

My 4 years of teaching at another high school and 2 years at a school in the Rochester area gave me room to spread my wings and put that cooperating teacher's techniques into practice. I felt good about what I was doing. I enjoyed interaction with teenagers. I felt I was accomplishing my goal of helping youngsters to learn and be prepared for life.

TEN YEAR HIATUS—four sons.

I can honestly say my return to teaching was like closing the door on what my prior teaching goals and achievements had been.

The ... District seemed to regress while the rest of the teaching world moved on. Included in their ultra-traditional program were:

• class grouping levels—regular, advanced, modified;

• tight department supervision—planbooks adhere to curriculum, discipline as a priority, lengthy observation reports which emphasized full account of every move teachers made;

• use of district curriculum guides which forced teachers from many schools to follow one set of rules for teaching writing;

• lack of media material;

• restraints placed on using media materials according to teacher's decisions. (Only two movies can be shown a year in English classes).

I succombed [sic] to the "rules," closed my classroom door, and did as much as I could in my own way, without jeopardizing my career. I've found the waves of paper-work which sweep over teachers kept me from thinking about new methods I would like to try.

Sarah:

Over the years, I have taught a full range of classes ... in the glory days of the late 60s and early 70s when I only had four classes and a period for conferences ... students were much easier to control. They were diligent and quiet; they were respectful and used to sitting and listening. It was a goal of mine in those days to get students to raise their hands and participate in the discussion. Things were so quiet! How things have changed! Along about that time, individualized instruction was the rage along with learning packets, and I devised a learning packet on poetry.

When I returned to teaching after a maternity leave, the district writing guide had been written and installed as "the way" to teach, along with marking period lists of activities to be completed, so creativity went out the window in favor of lock-step teaching methods, and if you weren't teaching the writing guide word for word during your observation, it was duly noted and criticized.

You have to get the kids to buy in ... to take a stake in it ... there are a lot of kids in those classes who are learning and I would like to have them learn more and I would like the other ones to start to learn instead of wasting time. It is such a shame when years go by and they lose their smartness almost because they develop the skill of shutting things out.

Both accounts evidence discrepancies between what these women had intended to achieve and how circumstances had hindered them, and many others. Top-down directives discouraged innovation and passing fads pushed teachers in one direction or another without sufficient training for follow through. No sooner had one idea been introduced and tried, than another replaced the first before anything could be absorbed or internalized and incorporated into more effective teaching and learning. After enough of these imposed fads occurred, many teachers had been turned around full circle! No wonder the metaphor of a cycle developed to describe attempts at educational reform!

Reform efforts now recognize that "teacher leadership roles should be constructed so that they convey positive, enabling attitudes and assumptions about teachers, about the nature of learning, about what we hope for our students" (Wasley, 1991, p. 162).

Students as Learners.   Through the years, students have felt restricted, too. If they questioned why they had to learn something, they were told, not shown, that it would be relevant later in life. If they suggested alternatives, students had to contend with time-conscious, harried teachers who felt compelled to cover curriculum that squelched many original ideas and forfeited teachable moments.

Student teachers, especially, find themselves caught in the middle. They must meet requirements for college courses and state certification, as well as balance the needs of their students with the cooperating teacher's concerns. Amid all these pressures, they strive to find ways of expressing their own intentions. One student teacher described her consternation in a learning log:

> I was concerned though, with the complete lack of feedback I got from M____. Before I taught, I was a bit reluctant to tell her of the activity I planned because based on what she had said before, I knew that she assumed I would simply copy her lessons on the days that I wasn't being observed.
>
> So, this is why my lesson today, even though it was by no means innovative seemed to rock her boat a little, because it is now clearer to her that I want to try new things for myself, and not just to please my supervisor.

Like so many others in education, this student teacher faced unnecessary objections to following her goals. External demands, not always educationally sound, divert teachers and students from fulfilling individual intentions that do possess merit. Learners and their interest in learning deserve more respect.

The irony behind these examples is the unintended lessons that are learned. Strong intentions may get sidetracked, but definitely reassert themselves. Just as Lorraine and Sarah sought assistance, this student teacher invented ways to circumvent pointless naysaying. Instead of having the freedom to openly try new ideas, they had to buck the system to be themselves.

Students do the same. Some daydream. Some act out. Others play the game only to a point. In myriad ways, students express dissatisfaction with having intentions foiled or totally ignored. Whether unconsciously or intentionally, they are ingenious in devising ways to obtain attention, positive or negative, to distract the teacher, so few goals are met.

One friendly, outgoing, ninth-grade boy volunteered to be interviewed and admitted in a one-on-one chat:

> I learn by communicating more and telling people how I feel about things we learn in class .... When you don't communicate more, you just sit there and get bored and remember feeling bored and that's why kids cut.

What a waste of creativity and energy! Superficial restraints cause resistance. *If only* all that energy of acting out was constructively channeled toward learning. *If only* learners could communicate and pursue interests. Cooperative efforts can establish reasonable and joint intentions to promote a productive climate for learning.

Joint Intentions.   Teachers who acknowledge learner intentions set the stage for incorporating individual perspectives for the good of the whole. Joint curriculum design encourages teachers to discuss plans with students right from the beginning of a lesson, unit, or course, so everyone gains ownership. Opportunities to develop individual pathways and common ground intensify inquiry for each learner—student and teacher alike. Benefits accrue over time.

How do you establish your intentions? How often do students indicate the directions they would like to take in pursuit of learning?

A fusion of intentions gives students voice, shapes cooperative action, and heightens individual interest. For example, I sometimes introduce a unit by brainstorming with students to uncover what they want to know about the topic. We list all ideas on the board. Inevitably, students name key points and add intriguing angles. We search for patterns to map out an overview and subtopics that graphically multiply options. Consequent student research and presentations reveal that, in the end, students learn basic information in order to pursue the breadth and depth of self-selected topics built on that knowledge.

Joint curriculum design repeatedly reaffirms the rejuvenating spirit of collaboration.

Perceptions—Learner Impressions

Student Input. After all these years in teaching, I am still amazed by student docility. Why don't they argue for more meaningful use of their time? Twelve years is a major part of anyone's life. I have always admired the few students who have challenged the system, but have rued the fact that they are so few and have such little impact. I believe students must be able to verbalize perceptions in all classes on a regular basis.

Recently, one eighth grader cautioned a class of student teachers seeking perspective:

> Students don't like to be singled out. Groups are okay, but if the same person always acts as leader, that person feels embarrassed and other students feel stupid.

Her words brought back memories of my first year of teaching, when I asked a class of tenth graders to evaluate my work. I learned a lesson back then that I still take to heart. Those I had unintentionally favored emphatically told me to avoid favoritism.

Joint curriculum design embraces individual differences, builds on learner strengths and interests, and utilizes hands-on experiences to promote sense-making for all students as equally important members of a learning community—based on collaboration and communication.

Differences in age, experience, and perspective characterize student–teacher relationships. Uncovering perceptions allows for a better rapport and more productive learning environment.

Cross-Purposes. Students react; they are rarely proactive. This approach is often mistaken for apathy or disinterest, instead of being recognized as ingrained—the result of treatment over time. Ideas each learner may have been free to follow in kindergarten become stifled in the regimentation of each succeeding school year. The cumulative effect is one of powerlessness.

Teachers react, too. Without considering school from the student's vantage point, they may judge students harshly. Some of the best teachers describe procedures that force, rather than lure, students to accomplish. Less effective teachers fall into the blame game, labelling students as lazy or rebellious. Teachers' perceptions can become just as skewed as students'.

The beginning of a school year proffers an excellent example of cross purposes that result from unexamined perceptions. A teacher often sets down rules the first day of class, unaware of impressions students receive. Students move from one class to another, listening to others tell them how to behave and what they will do for the rest of the term. Is it any wonder that teachers feel drained and bright-eyed youth feel deadened by the end of the day!

This one-way communication establishes extrinsic rewards and not only disregards, but also squelches individual and intrinsic incentives for teachers and students. In contrast, joint curriculum design invites two-way communication to uncover student interest and increase involvement. If you discuss the overarching ideas that frame a course, students can help shape a syllabus, a tool sadly lacking in high school. Too often, without an overview, students face each course as one task after another, whereas teachers feel exasperated because students seem bored or disinterested. Common understandings of course goals unite everyone.

Influence of Impressions.   The power of perceptions marked the start of our study when Lorraine and Sarah thought they would only involve well-behaved classes. We discussed whether classes that accepted teacher control and therefore succeeded by following rules would resist change. Perhaps less cooperative classes disliked the kind of teaching they had been receiving. Would they be more ripe for change? At the possibility of working with the more restless classes, Lorraine replied:

> I like the 5th period better, so it's hard for me to make a choice. When you like a class better, you can't really make a fair choice … But you may feel that (3rd period)'s better for me to learn on when I have to struggle ….

> The 3rd period is kind of erratic. I felt I had to introduce you to them because they're apt to say, "Who's that woman?" in the middle of class. Or, say, "What's she doing here?" or "What's she writing?" … I thought one boy might interrupt and I wanted to do it on my own grounds.

I was struck by her response. After years of administrative control, Lorraine assumed I expected her to struggle, as if improving teaching strategies needed to be a test or crucible. Closely related to this perception was her conscious determination to maintain a measure of authority that she felt was necessary for learning to occur. I held a contrasting view. Trying new methods poses some stress, but need not be nerve wracking! Observant students curious enough to ask questions held promise for a study that sought their input.

Sarah, too, revealed a different sense from mine. At the suggestion of working with a more restless class, Sarah claimed, "I don't want to be so vulnerable, to try something new with students who don't want to cooperate, but who will turn everything into fun and games."

Why not inject a spirit of fun and games? Why not lighten the mood for both teaching and learning? Students have felt victorious when they succeed in making a serious teacher smile.

We considered compromise—Include both cooperative and restless classes? This possibility prompted Sarah to write:

> With Period 7 ... it's hard enough to get that class to do something .... Now, I'm thinking I have this resistance because I want them to go my way and they don't want to go that way—so if I had another way to make them go, it would be easier .... Maybe it would be good to give them a more positive attitude .... I never get to the loose or easy stage because I'm keeping a tight rein to keep control, to keep them with me.

These discussions raised other serious issues regarding perceptions. Underlying assumptions began to surface. As we analyzed their existence and influence, we strengthened the bonds of collaboration and trust among ourselves and shed some self-imposed restraints.

Overcoming stagefright, Lorraine and Sarah decided to include all four classes. They wanted to see if joint curriculum design would work as well for both cooperative and restless classes. Past experiences led me to believe the risk was far less than they suspected.

What perceptions affect your decisions? How do students respond to your view of their capabilities?

Expectations—Learner Potential

Students are typecast and live up to labels. If they are not expected to succeed, why would they bother to try? Conversely, if they are expected to perform beyond their abilities, they quickly lose faith in themselves out of frustration. However, if reasonably high expectations are set, students strive to achieve them.

Joint curriculum design urges students and teachers to aim high, but more important, to articulate these goals. Students need to recognize and develop potential and teachers need to expand strategies to support student efforts. Positive beliefs become self-fulfilling.

Adolescent Learners. Joint curriculum design addresses the special needs of adolescents. Learners construct personalized meaning through interaction with others. They gain independence through acknowledging individual differences, identifying strengths, thinking critically, and making decisions. As they debrief, they study consequences to refine judgment.

As Egan (1990) explained, adolescents deal with powerful affective surges as they strive to make sense of the world:

> [In their] capacity to form associations with people, things, institutions, or rather with the transcendent human qualities that can be embodied in, or projected into, such people, things, institutions, or whatever ... certain selected things stand out bright and clear and somewhat larger than life. (p. 127)

Without perspective, adolescents may misconstrue or distort information. The world may appear dull and ideas may seem static if students receive information, rather than arrive at knowledge through imaginative associations and multiple understandings. Egan urged teachers to embue learning with metaphor and narrative, with enthusiasm and wonder, to tap adolescent capacities beyond traditional, rational lines of thought. Joint curriculum design encourages this affective and cognitive growth through collaboration.

In addition, Egan decried the kind of schooling that left adolescents with "little sense of what ideas are or how to use them and control them" (p. 225); he argued for a reflective and exploratory curriculum to encourage "the development of fluency in dealing with ideas" (p. 225). To embrace logical and psychological awarenesses, social and cultural contingencies, he concluded:

> If we do not stimulate their sense of wonder, we leave adolescent students victims of an intensity of boredom in schools, and the victims of any kind of sensation out of it. If this aspect of romance is not properly developed, students fall easily into various forms of cynicism. (p. 219)

Joint curriculum design taps into the resources of "romantic understanding" that Egan described. Students anticipate learning and express themselves more fully in an atmosphere that welcomes genuine, unique responses to original discoveries or seemingly disappointing turns. Diverse learners support each other in a holistic, inductive pursuit of knowledge.

Relevance. Relevance for adolescents in educational offerings has been a major issue since the beginnings of compulsory education. Progressive alternatives have persistently materialized in reaction to traditional public schooling. Constantly changing social needs have caused educators to revise some goals, but reformers still struggle with how best to incorporate the richness of diversity and its tremendous influence on literacy and identity (Delpit, 1989; Ferdman, 1990), especially for adolescents. Acknowledging the importance of access to the "power code" competes with preserving cultural differences.

In response, progressives urge educators to engage students to "ask powerful, critical questions and seek alternative explanations" (Perrone, 1991, p. 13). They seek ways to honor diversity, not develop polarizations (Carini, 1991). They stress the ironies of an educational system that touts individual thinking, but operates in conforming and constricting fashion.

If we prevent adolescents from exercising choice and recognizing consequences, how can we expect sustained inquiry, construction of knowledge, divergent thinking?

Underestimating Potential. At the same time, students need more exposure to career choices. Non-college-bound students often lack hands-on schooling until they reach ninth or tenth grade. This situation leaves restless middle school students floundering for years and losing faith in themselves as learners. When school expectations do not allow for personal strengths, students feel inadequate and act out to express individual identities. One twelfth-grade boy, training for carpentry, told a meeting of concerned school and community curriculum planners:

> I didn't do good in school until I went to vo-tech. Once I went to vo-tech, I really liked it and took math more seriously and took better notes since I knew it would help me on the job.

In another situation, I have introduced low-academic-achieving seniors to research. Many had never been given the chance to use school library resources though this was their twelfth year of public education! The librarian expressed doubts about their abilities to behave and to succeed. With guidance, these students pursued topics of interest—cars, body-building, carpentry, cosmetics. They appreciated their new-found ability to track down information. *Consumer Reports* amazed them. They never knew such a publication existed. How long these students had been denied their rights! High expectations yielded high results.

Similarly, teacher expectations have also been foiled or delayed. Many teachers, like Lorraine and Sarah, strove to make a difference by attending conferences and reading professional journals. Many ideas seemed worthwhile, but implementation proved difficult because (a) administrators lacked knowledge or interest in supporting change, and (b) ideas lacked connections, causing fragmentary, isolated attempts.

In the absence of opportunities for teachers and students to grow came such situations as those described as *Horace's Compromise* (Sizer, 1985), in which teachers agreed to join students in the "conspiracy of the least." According to this form of tacit bargaining, teachers and students did not challenge one another to achieve, but merely went through daily motions of mindless routines that passed for teaching and learning. Stagnation foiled active pursuit of knowledge.

Joint curriculum design offers an alternative route to rectify past constraints and to revitalize teaching. Collaborative efforts with colleagues and students break the former futility of piecemeal efforts and ensure a coherent and dynamic process, highlighting expectations by capitalizing on individual differences.

Self-Actualizing Goals. Teachers model individual growth when they design professional development plans and work consistently toward self-actualizing goals. Joint curriculum design suggests that teachers enlist students in the process, to enable students to identify personal, educational goals. Together, they work toward fulfillment.

Present school structures that curtail forward thinking can change. For example, Sizer's (1985) idea of longer class periods has developed into *block* or *intensive* scheduling. This alteration of a traditional school structure signals greater belief in learner ability to concentrate for longer time spans and to delve deeper into course content. This change also raises expectations for teachers to learn strategies to make extended sessions exciting, not just more of the same.

Joint curriculum design can create schools that cause teachers and students to be independent thinkers who exert critical and creative capacities to tackle present problems and design effective and innovative solutions.

What expectations do you share with students? How do student expectations become part of daily lessons and long-range projects?

Reactions—Learner Feedback, Achievement, Satisfaction

Joint curriculum design is predicated on action research that demands reflection about teaching practice and consequent learning in order for effective change to occur. Student reactions to classroom actions indicate the impact of a philosophy of teaching. To determine the success of teaching, classroom events must be measured according to feedback. Test scores alone offer insufficient information.

What kinds of feedback are exchanged? What specific achievements occur? How satisfied are students with the end results?

Generally, students want to please parents, teachers, and themselves. They seek approval of their ideas and efforts, at the same time that they are trying to assert independence. Unfortunately, even the best intentioned adults, whose purpose is to show teenagers how capable they can be, end up criticizing student work too strenuously. Adolescents often feel overwhelmed unless encouragement accompanies comments.

Constructive criticism facilitates improvement when given in a positive vein and accompanied by suggestions about how to improve. Rather than focus on deficiencies or weaknesses, specific feedback regarding strengths informs students what actions to perform, rather than avoid, to achieve positive results (Engstrom, 1993). Inductive questioning inspires individual insight. Student confidence grows amid fair and honest feedback.

Joint curriculum design flows from frequent polling of students. Interim evaluations allow for immediate changes that benefit the class, as opposed to final evaluations that serve future classes. I ask for specific feedback about what activities have been effective and what topics students would like to pursue further. Student satisfaction and sense of achievement are integral to a productive, learning climate.

These evaluations include peer and self-assessment. I not only ask for feedback on my actions, but also ask students to describe their contributions. How prepared have they been? What readings and activities did they complete? How much have they participated in classwork and discussions? Review reinforces responsibility.

Approaching students to obtain their reactions cues them to the extent to which you care about their level of satisfaction, as well as their capacity to succeed.

Joint curriculum design depends on open exchange. Students and teachers need to express reactions in an atmosphere of trust and reciprocal listening to balance individual needs with group ends.

SUMMARY

This chapter differentiated traditional teaching from progressive learning, placing **joint curriculum design** within the extremes of these two educational orientations. It suggested ways to verbalize a philosophy of education to analyze how closely actions and intentions match, before gathering student feedback.

Behind-the-Scenes Mental Preparation: Suggestions for Learning Log Entries

1. Select the one class with which you wish to employ **joint curriculum design**. Identify the actions you take and the reasons why you proceed in that fashion. List your intentions, perceptions, and expectations. Describe observable student reactions.

2. Consider the other classes you teach. Give specific reasons why you would not begin with each. If there is an individual or group of students influencing this choice, write the drawbacks that you believe occasion this decision.

3. Decide how you will collect feedback from students. Determine the kinds of information you seek and prepare how you will explain the purpose to students.

On-Stage Try-outs:
Collaborative Efforts to Ascertain Needs

1. Discuss with students the possibility of sharing decision-making about coursework. Solicit ideas and issues from students and list for future reference.

2. Ask students to describe in writing changes they would like to see. Encourage them to discuss the assignment at home and to include comments from family. Collect papers to review and share results with students.

4

Setting the Tone: Environmental Factors

ଚଠ ◆ ଚଃ

Environmental factors set the tone for learning. Influences of space and time can create an atmosphere conducive to inquiry and collaboration.

PERSON–ENVIRONMENT FIT

Every theater evokes response. A Broadway stage suggests a more formal and distant audience involvement than a theater-in-the-round. An outdoor stage creates a certain informality, whereas a cabaret implies intimacy. So too, every classroom sets a tone and offers clues about what learners can expect.

A teacher's use of classroom space indicates a conception of learning (Gifford, 1987). Podiums, lecterns, and raised platforms at the front of a room prefigure traditional teaching. Worktables, movable seats, and resource centers indicate more progressive approaches. Upon entering a classroom, students immediately discern messages from the physical layout. These impressions translate into feelings of personal comfort and expected behavior (Ittelson, 1973). A positive, welcoming atmosphere signals a productive person–environment fit.

A philosophy of education shapes decisions regarding classroom (a) seating, (b) activities, (c) control, (d) press, and (e) pace (see Fig. 4.1). These factors influence perceptions, expectations, intentions, actions, and reactions (as discussed in chapter 3).

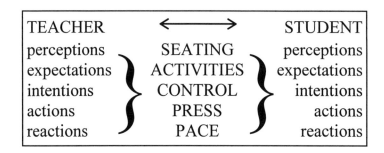

FIG. 4.1. Classroom environment factors that reflect student and teacher actions and attitudes.

What classroom climate prevails? Do physical characteristics create positive and motivating forces? Do thinkers predominate, or are students acceptingly passive? How do classroom structures support goals?

Seating arrangements and consequent activities prompt behaviors in relation to control factors, interpersonal distances, and instructional pace. With **joint curriculum design**, teachers and students play complementary roles that demonstrate connections among educational goals, classroom structures, and content delivery.

Seating—Room Arrangements

Interior decorators design a room so people feel welcome. They focus particularly on available seating. Does furniture invite someone to sit down or are seats turned away from the entrance? Do chairs encourage conversation or stand in isolation to separate and divide? These concepts transfer to the classroom.

What messages do seating arrangements imply?

Upon entering a traditional classroom, students sense that action will be limited. Seated in rows and columns, they fall into line, one behind the other, subject to the authority figure at the front of the room. Like a large, formal theater, this arrangement treats students as a passive audience. Furthermore, row and column seating affects student interest and patterns of interaction (Koneya, 1976). The level of student participation correlates with proximity to the teacher. Those seated in the first few rows pay more attention. Students out of the teacher's view and facing the backs of others' heads lack incentive to concentrate. Daydreamers and off-task students tend to be seated at a distance from the action. Thus, assigned seating unintentionally limits student involvement.

In my supervisory experience, I have observed long, narrow classrooms, in which students sat seven deep. From the fourth row back, interest and accessibility waned. After changing the room around by a 90° angle so no student sat further back than four seats, teachers discovered that student attention increased and distractions diminished.

One student teacher I supervised chose to seat pairs of seventh graders, not in double columns that would still imply regimentation, but in alternating patterns, which signaled and evoked teamwork. He explained:

> Partners tend to concentrate upon their tasks in a more relaxed manner. They seem less interested in what others are doing. They have more room to stretch their legs and spread out their belongings. I don't always use this seating, but they like it when I do.

In contrast, circular seating arrangements capitalize on nonverbal communication to heighten participation (Heyman, 1978). As students become clearly visible to one another, nonverbal cues indicate reason to be alert. As a result, acting more like a company of players, the class becomes more attuned to the group, more inclined to listen and respond. This seating suggests a seminar approach that encourages everyone to contribute to discussions. Like a small theater, this setting becomes more intimate and personal.

Some teachers find a circle uncomfortable, especially at first. If they do not sit with students, they literally don't know where to turn! Keeping one space open facilitates movement, but they still feel awkward. Actually sitting with students is more indicative of the level playing field a circle suggests. Discussions conducted in the round include everyone.

Two variations of the circle group students according to task. The horseshoe formation directs attention toward the opening for presentations, boardwork, films, or overhead projections. The opposing sides approach splits the seating in half, creating a confrontational stance, effective for debates. However, either of these variations prove to be compromises, reducing the amount of face-to-face student interaction because available space generally requires double or triple rows, depending on room specifications.

Yet another possibility rests in what Totten (1985) described as a "fluid setting," in which pairing and grouping of students remain flexible. By shifting membership according to task, teachers raise expectations for students to participate. As more students become actively engaged, peer pressure and teacher movement encourage everyone to perform at his or her best. When lessons incorporate shifting small group activities, students shuffle themselves on a regular basis among random or selected groupings, which prompts them to exchange viewpoints and broaden understandings.

Figure 4.2 illustrates five configurations. These illustrations account for 28 seats each, yet the number of seats does not appear the same. Similar impressions occur in the classroom. Rows and columns create a feeling of crowdedness that a circle dispels. Horseshoe or opposing sides direct attention outward, whereas, alternating pairs evokes a feeling of partnership. Thus, seating arrangements send clear, tacit messages.

What seating arrangements have you tried? How much freedom do students have to move around the room? How much time do students spend on task?

At the start of our study, Sarah rotated students in row and column seating on a regular basis. Lorraine, too, assigned seats. Later, collaboration with students and cooperative learning strategies dispelled uniformity, making seating plans superfluous. (See chapters 5 and 6.)

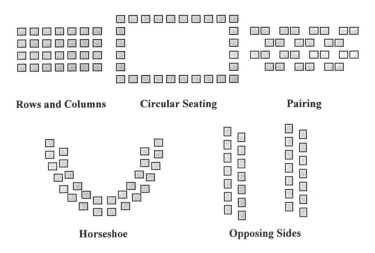

Rows and Columns   **Circular Seating**   **Pairing**

Horseshoe   **Opposing Sides**

FIG. 4.2. Five classroom seating arrangements.

Activity—Congruence

Seating arrangements provide more than interior decorating tips; they set the tone for possible activities within the physical dimensions of a room.

If left to chance or habit, classrooms assume a character that dictates routines and patterns of behavior that can quickly become stale. Diverse use of space transforms surroundings. Flexible seating arrangements aid learning when seating varies according to intended actions.

Traditional seating arrangements promote a teacher-directed activity structure that discourages student involvement. The typical pattern of talk that develops entails IRE or teacher initiation–student reply–teacher elaboration (Cazden, 1988). In addition, teachers tend to answer student questions, rather than encourage student interaction. The dynamics of this setting often unwittingly curtail student expression.

In contrast, circular seating arrangements invite exchange. A teacher who sits on the same physical level as students joins in the learning community, eliciting student prior knowledge, gaining insight into student potential, and orchestrating student interaction. Student interest and input increase as they respond to the presence of peers and the opportunity to express ideas. In this setting, a teacher reaffirms individual thought and elevates the role of the student. Consequently, a teacher can utilize student knowledge bases and interests to invite further inquiry, and students recognize the importance of substantiating opinions.

Small-group activities present other ways to engage students. Designated roles and responsibilities create an interdependence (Johnson & Johnson, 1991). Positioned to face each other to work jointly on a task, students sense a shift toward greater expectations to contribute, question, comment, and clarify. The level of thought and accountability escalates. Small-group activities broaden social and affective perspectives, as well as cognitive gains. Cooperative learning tasks cause students to recognize each other's strengths, delegate individual responsibilities, and learn how to work well with others.

Varied activity structures serve multiple purposes. For example, as new students enter a class, they often feel uncomfortable and self-conscious, particularly if English is not their first language. Within small groups, these students gain self-confidence by contributing views, at the same time that classmates overcome their own hesitancy or reserve in speaking with a stranger. Before a smaller audience, students give others greater attention and gain totally new insights.

The connection between seating arrangements and possible tasks seems so obvious, yet it is often overlooked. Varying classroom activities and groupings can enhance student performance.

How do physical structures support varied classroom assignments? How often do students form and re-form groups to complete tasks?

Control—Who's in Charge?

No classroom feature operates in isolation. Each aspect connects to another and the cumulative effect touches everyone present. Consider the interplay of concepts regarding seating and activity structures with the concept of control.

Control theory acknowledges that people ultimately control their own behavior. Glasser (1986) applied control theory to the classroom, where he identified needs for belonging, freedom, and power as the sources of motivation. He argued that students prefer to act and choose, rather than react. Therefore, he urged teachers to encourage student choice so that acting and thinking would become more free and voluntary which, in turn, would lead to more effective learning.

Integral to joint curriculum design, Glasser's theory sparked many discussions in my collaborations. After reading his work, Lorraine reported:

> From *Control Theory in the Classroom*, I gleaned that no one does anything simple or complex, because someone tells them to do it. Discipline is only a problem when students are forced into classes where they do not experience satisfaction. Criticism is the most destructive blow to our egos. We store satisfying pictures in our heads of an activity we remember as pleasant. The reverse is true of unpleasant (dissatisfying) pictures. These pictures motivate us or turn us off. We can change our pictures—a caring school person can help change a student's learning pictures if tangible, in-class satisfaction is experienced.

These realizations led her to consider the messages suggested by classroom seating and learning activities in terms of the concept of control. Traditional classrooms, "hierarchical and ritualistic," leave students to be "seen as ignorant, with little status and few rights" (Bernstein, 1975, p. 98). With the teacher in complete control, students lack freedom or power. In addition, this approach tends to "discourage connections with everyday realities ... makes of educational knowledge something not ordinary or mundane, but something esoteric" (Bernstein, p. 99). Remoteness of content increases the distancing caused by subordinate placement. Is it surprising then that students often feel inferior, uncomfortable, apathetic in such settings?

In contrast, acknowledgement of individual worth engenders a sense of belonging that inspires more focused interest and induces more student-to-student questioning and response. By sharing control, a teacher acts like a facilitator, generating open-ended activities. Students inevitably introduce topics and resources that provoke thought, enrich investigations, and challenge classmates.

After reading Glasser's book, Sarah commented:

> I was intrigued by the chapter about the five needs ... I like this idea of importance, belonging ... a lot of things I thought of in my own life that I felt in the schools I went to were taken away from me. ... Things I try to give back to the students because from my own life experience seeing I thought it was necessary ... I wanted the students to feel the power of having a sense of competence.

Independence does make a difference. Teacher-controlled classrooms tend to hamper student expression and impede active learning, whereas *shared control fosters student responsibility for learning*. I have repeatedly found that students who are given the freedom to work alone or with others to complete assignments feel empowered to make decisions while learning to face the consequences of their choices and actions.

Joint curriculum design involves the willingness of teachers to credit student initiative and curiosity. This, in turn, stretches students to use their potential. This switch from traditional roles takes time, practice, and patience to achieve. Many veteran and student teachers with whom I have collaborated have struggled to develop the means to share control with students.

If the goal of education is to develop lifelong learners, why reserve control of learning for teachers and thereby obstruct student responsibility, progress, accountability? As Glasser

(1986) argued, people ultimately control their own behavior. **How then can teachers believe that they do control classrooms full of people whose minds naturally wander and whose levels of understanding differ?**

Establishing an aura of authority only gives the appearance of control. Steadfastly holding to such an illusion fails to challenge students to take control of their own learning.

Press—Is There Room to Grow?

Besides the issues of control, other unspoken but keenly felt aspects of surroundings either nurture or thwart pursuit of knowledge. *Proxemics*, or the study of one's use of space, addresses this whole other dimension of the teaching–learning environment: press.

Press involves how people respond to settings in terms of perceived comfort levels evoked from verbal and nonverbal cues. Each of us maintains a subjective understanding of personal and interpersonal distance. In his classic work, Hall (1966) suggested that people operate in at least four distance zones (intimate, personal, social, and public), with each zone understood in relation to culture, status, personality, and environment.

As we size up one another, we tend to surround ourselves with invisible boundaries that we expect others will not trespass. We use surroundings, body language, and symbolic messages to communicate with one another. We position ourselves according to desired degrees of interaction. Yet, the circumference of these invisible lines varies from individual to individual, group to group. What one person (or culture) considers a polite distance, another considers encroaching or isolating. Few classrooms allow for this reality. Unintentional tensions develop unnecessarily if the degree of human press inhibits learners.

Traditional classrooms signal individual, competitive climates that run contrary to the need for acceptance and belonging, especially strong among adolescents. In contrast, more fluid classrooms, which facilitate student interaction, address these needs. The tenor of the classroom relies heavily on these underlying logistics of interpersonal space.

Crowding is another derivative of press. Freedman (1975) studied urban areas in terms of crowding and found that the sense of encroachment results not only from the space between people, but also from "the formality of the relationship and the setting" (pp. 71–72). His ideas transfer easily to the context of the classroom, where connections between control and press become obvious in the rapport that exists between the teacher and the class. Crowding may be psychological, as well as physical. Where teachers act as experts and students are relegated to subordinate positions, distance prevails. Where teachers build a community of learners, students draw together, more willing to learn from one another.

This concept of press arose when one of Sarah's eighth graders could fidget no matter what seat she gave him. He found ways to converse with anyone, anywhere in the room. After his class complained about arranged seating and Sarah allowed more mobility, this student staked out his own comfort zone, stretched his legs, and attended to classwork—no longer distracting others.

Thus, press encompasses each individual's sense of personal space and interpersonal distance, in relation to room arrangements and class activity structures. The power of press can sharpen learner attitudes and reactions. Another factor is the element of time.

Pace—What Time Is It, Anyway?

Individual biological rhythms and peak times vary for "day" or "night" people. Some people "merely exist" at certain hours, but describe themselves as "alert" and "productive" during other time periods. In addition, individuals are quick to explain that they need *more* or *less* time to complete some task—a reality that either hurries them up or slows them down when required to work at some externally determined rate of speed.

Though we readily agree on how much we all differ, schooling functions as though we are clones of one another. Of necessity, any institution requires organization, but the rationale behind some practices deserves reconsideration.

Do practices improve the quality of work? Is there sufficient time to understand assignments prior to attempting them? Is appropriate feedback provided at interim points of effort? How do practices relate to assessment?

These questions and more revolve around the often mismanaged idea of pacing. **Pacing** constitutes the amount of time allotted for completion of tasks. Most classrooms operate as if everyone required the same amount of time to solve a problem, read an excerpt, or write a response. This attitude neglects learning styles (Gardner, 1991) or individual needs for guidance in how to best approach a task and achieve competence.

When pace predominates, students either manage to maintain an arbitrary pace or lose their footing. Those who need less time become restless waiting for others to catch up; those who need more time feel flustered when lagging behind. Loss of interest or self-esteem skews the reality that a different time frame could offer.

If pacing and purposes conflict, confusion reigns. Content coverage does not equate with comprehension. A set pace disregards individual differences, forfeiting further student inquiry or interpretation. With a clearer understanding of the impact of pacing, a teacher can plan sufficient leeway to encourage learners to concentrate more fully, ask more questions, probe deeper.

Doyle (1977) identified multidimensionality, simultaneity, and unpredictability as the most salient features of a classroom. These features all add value to the learning process. However, Doyle also found that unsuccessful teachers tried to reduce the natural complexity by ignoring multiplicity and simultaneity. Sadly, this approach limits and constrains. Setting a pace merely for a semblance of stability stifles individual thought and learner interaction with the material and each other.

Pacing ties in directly with the concept of control. Grannis (1980) noted that teacher-dominated instruction made "minimal demands on students' critical, creative, or empathic capacities" (p. 46). He further explained, "the form that the teacher fosters conveys knowledge about knowledge" (p. 54). The focus becomes a display of teacher knowledge, unquestionably definitive, and a loss of student motivation or inquiry. Daily repetition of this approach undermines learning. To belabor points students already know or skim over important ideas they do not grasp complicates learning.

Joint curriculum design invites teachers to negotiate time limits with students and adjust through frequent time checks. With support, students learn to structure tasks and manage time to achieve success. To recognize varying rates inspires persistence. Motivation to succeed increases when the prospect seems attainable.

FREEING UP SPACE

Stage directors know how to transform the smallest stage into a set that suggests wide-ranging possibilities in the minds of those present. Teachers free up space in the classroom by crediting student interest in learning. Joint curriculum design values brainstorming with students to foster active involvement and individual input throughout the learning process. This approach relies on conscious attention to intangibles.

The relationship among the intangibles illustrated in Fig. 4.3 is interdependent. Willingness and ability to develop joint **purposes** assumes **trust** and **flexibility**. The **boundaries** and **consensus** flow from mutual feelings of acceptance and from ownership in joint decision-making.

Purposes—Individual and Common Goals

Why? This question underlies every action. Without a reason, why begin, much less continue or complete anything? **Purposes** provide specific rationales for proceeding with some course of action. Without clear statement of intentions little can be accomplished. Goal setting has always been essential to teaching.

How often are goals and implementation of curriculum assessed? Student turnover from one semester or year to the next can inspire teachers to take stock and adjust. Trends can cause

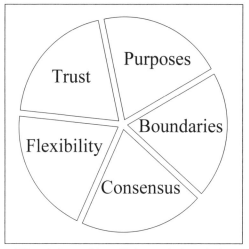

FIG. 4.3. Intangibles of joint curriculum design.

changes in content or methodology. Researching educational theories and practices can further inform teachers. But actually spelling out and reconsidering purposes for teaching can be enlightening. Apple (1990) urged teachers to study their choices, to pinpoint "hidden curriculum," and to eradicate areas that precluded critical analysis of material and method.

How often are students consulted? Joint curriculum design encourages regular review of topics and emphases by students and teachers. A curriculum that denies this opportunity to challenge the status quo underestimates learners and obscures learning.

How often does a teacher write out a personal philosophy of education? A philosophy of education proffers a teacher a personal statement in time. A regular review makes it a working document from which a teacher can continually take stock and improve, charting new directions along the way. Successful teachers set achievable goals and develop ways to attain them. Reflectivity on past performance and consideration of future practice empowers a teacher (Giroux, 1988; Schon, 1987, 1990). **How often does a teacher compare lesson planbooks in light of educational philosophy?**

Joint curriculum design includes collaboration with students in reviewing goals and lessons. Without common understanding, teachers and students often work at odds with one another. In my experience, most teachers and students hold similar educational goals, but usually fail to discuss them. Teachers wish to impart knowledge and instill a drive for learning; students seek knowledge that holds their interest and has relevance to their lives. Teachers and students wish for greater exchange of ideas, higher levels of thought, more originality and creativity. Unfortunately, teachers and students rarely know how closely their hopes resemble one another.

Joint curriculum design includes students in the reflective process. When polled, students are more than willing to describe experiences—both positive and negative. As Lorraine and Sarah learned, students possess perspectives that are often unimagined by the teacher. (See chapter 5.)

Flexibility—Options

Flexibility requires an ability to adapt to new, different, or changing avenues of thought or action. In learning situations, teachers introduce or elaborate on a topic; students uniquely receive, react, and respond to the information. Flow of ideas multiplies in accordance with the number of listeners, but the richness is often lost in the student silence that accompanies IRE or teacher talk. To raise interest and thinking levels, both teachers and students need to activate spontaneity.

Switching from teacher-determined classrooms to jointly negotiated learning environments requires a willing give-and-take on the part of teachers and students. Planning is essential, but so is the ability to go with the flow, to recognize a teachable moment and pounce on it. Strict adherence to beautifully written plans may miss the point and lose the learner.

With joint curriculum design, teachers and students balance a common grasp of goals with active listening and contributing to class dialogue. Establishing joint purposes relies on a spirit of flexibility that dignifies divergent thinking and acknowledges unforeseen avenues of thought. Rather than fear *interruptions*, students explore tangents they would otherwise hesitate to broach. Some excellent ideas surface under these conditions.

Trust—Individual Voice

Trust encompasses concepts of caring, confidence, and acceptance—the belief that thoughts, feelings, and opinions will be heard and respected. In the classroom, a climate of trust builds student confidence and develops intrinsic motivation that activates student desire to achieve. Bruner (1966) attested to the value of trust in the learning process. He stressed that "emphasis upon individual responsibility and initiative, upon independence in decision and action, upon perfectability of self—all of these serve to perpetuate more basic competency motives" (p. 121).

A teacher who solicits student opinion and honors divergent thinking reassures students that more than one answer can address a question. Students learn to think for themselves when a teacher implies that they have worthwhile ideas to share. In a climate of trust, even the most controversial topics receive thoughtful airing.

If a teacher cares enough to listen attentively and responsively to students, students learn to imitate that behavior, to avoid jumping to conclusions or prejudging. A moral standard develops, demonstrating the value of each individual, the importance of listening and discerning differences, and the growth of thought. In the process, real dialogue occurs (Noddings, 1984).

Thus, joint curriculum design has repeatedly shown that the degree of student participation parallels the level of trust offered. Although many teachers fear that sharing control takes students off task, ironically, the opposite proves true. Given freedom to operate on their own, students often demand more of themselves and each other than teachers are generally wont to do (Gross, 1992a).

Boundaries—Limits

Joint curriculum design assumes that recognition of acceptable limits sustains a positive, cooperative climate and expedites constructive participation, but **boundaries** do need to be set. Teenagers are well versed in classroom operations. Their collective experiences comprise a body of knowledge worth investigating. Taking time to cull student outlooks often saves time that may be wasted later on *correcting* inappropriate behavior.

When they participate in drawing boundaries, students not only establish acceptable social behavior, they also question what is important to learn and how to proceed. Too often, students are left to rely solely on the teacher for direction. When they exercise choice, students learn to value individual accountability.

When goals are jointly designed and explicit, students also have a stake in meeting them. They are more willing to quell distracters in the interest of not wasting time. Applying the student as worker metaphor that Freire (1973) explored, with a clear purpose in mind, students want to get the job done. Ownership inspires student action and ingenuity to meet goals.

The roles of teachers and students change once these factors and their impact are acknowledged. (See chapter 8.) Students enjoy increased rights, but also learn the other side of freedom—responsibility. In a passive setting, students can blame a number of causes besides themselves for lack of success. In an active setting, students learn the limits of blame. They grasp not only the content, but also the effects of the social contract.

A teacher does need to assist students in the process because "students' conceptions of the alternatives in a situation depend on their past experiences and their perceptions of the situational constraints" (Johnson & Johnson, 1991, p. 15). As facilitator, you establish and shape areas for negotiation.

For example, change involves *permission*—to move around a classroom, to create workspaces, to confer with one another—actions not deemed acceptable in traditional settings. If permitted, students voluntarily restructure groups to gather opinions, clarify ideas, or verify information. At the same time, teachers find they adjust to new visions of the boundaries of classroom time and effort. A new noise level or more fluid movement of students can startle a teacher who has resigned herself to change but has not envisioned all of the ramifications!

A key aspect of joint curriculum design is the value of ongoing conversations regarding all of these changes and consequences. Interim assessments of all aspects of the learning process help to address or prevent glitches.

Consensus—Solidarity

The idea of student freedom can cause concerns for teachers and students. Will *necessary* information be given short shrift? How much decision making will be shared? The concept of joint curriculum design relies on building consensus.

Consensus connotes common judgment, solidarity, a united front. In the classroom, building consensus seems a utopian belief, particularly on the secondary level with heterogeneous groupings of seemingly apathetic teens. However, consensus is not so elusive. Once students are registered for a course, whether required or elective, they are obligated to be present. **Why not switch the tone from an obligation to a span of time in which to explore options within acceptable boundaries? A spirit of investigation overrides a sense of duty.**

Consensus develops as purposes are established and boundaries are clearly defined. Consensus assumes a solution and demonstrates a willingness to adapt and adopt. Diversity of opinion is expected, but so is the ability to resolve differences for the good of the whole.

If common goals remain prominent, *if* flexibility and trust are sustained, and *if* boundaries are maintained, consensus naturally follows. The success of joint curriculum design rests in these contingencies.

SUMMARY

Joint curriculum design is an exciting process because each party contributes to building an environment in which everyone enjoys ownership, rights, and responsibilities. Teachers and students understand the goals and the ground rules for meeting them in a flexible and trusting climate.

Behind-the-Scenes Mental Preparation: Suggestions for Learning Log Entries

1. Sketch your classroom and mark off the division of space used by you and your students. Study details to design alternative arrangements. Try different layouts every so often to see how space may be reconsidered.

2. Recall past successful lessons that did not rely on usual classroom arrangements. Describe the particular features that varied and describe student success. Project how to reuse or adapt previous successes.

3. Define trust, flexibility, or control in terms of students. Note any distinctions you make for age or ability. Question the grounds for those distinctions. Have you ever found the contrary to be true? How can you experiment with other possibilities?

On-Stage Tryouts: Collaborative Efforts Regarding Classroom Climate

1. Allow students to sit anywhere in the room and write down how they feel about learning from that chosen position. After a few minutes, ask students to reseat themselves anywhere in the room and explain how learning from that position would be different.

Divide students into groups to share their perceptions and arrive at some common insights.

Elicit group reports to share with the whole class. In the discussion, touch on issues of choice, trust, and control.

Consensus: Establish seating options.

2. Ask students to define *teaching* and *learning* and write *job descriptions* for teachers and learners.

Pair students to compare their ideas and solicit key distinctions.

Divide the class in half and have them role play job interviews—one teacher, one learner; then reverse role play parts.

Poll class for insights gained regarding assumptions and discuss the consequences of acting on assumptions.

Consensus: Define roles in joint goal setting.

5

Methods of Acting:
Messages and Meanings

ဆ ◆ �%

A review of specific contexts for methods of acting in light of philosophy, environment, and goals inspires new strategies for learning.

In theater, a cast reviews scripts for messages and meanings in order to envision an integral performance. In the classroom, actions and perceptions of students and teachers differ. Like a theater company, the class and teacher can achieve mutual understanding and effective learning if they discuss meanings derived from messages.

Joint curriculum design evolves from the realization that each class operates within a unique context. What succeeds for one may not work well for another. Lesson plans do not automatically transfer. Teachers who try to keep two sections on the same page strive for the elusive and frustrate themselves and students in the attempt.

Active communication between teachers and students clarifies messages and meanings to improve learning. Joint curriculum design resembles a mobile of elements (see chapter 2) that moves as a community of learners analyze how current **philosophy, environment,** and **goals** touch on **methods of learning.**

MESSAGES

Unlike most of the working world, secondary school teachers and students adjust to different sets of people throughout the day. A spirit and chemistry define each class. Switching from one period to

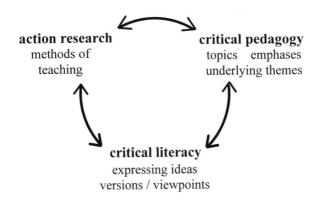

FIG. 5.1. Messages imbedded in learning contexts.

another, teachers and students shed the events of one group to face the next combination of people, ideas, and experiences.

Consequently, they play different parts several times a day, as they move from class to class.

Joint curriculum design urges teachers and students to examine the messages imbedded in contexts of learning. **Action research** studies **methods of teaching** for messages about plans for action. **Critical pedagogy** analyzes messages in **topics and emphases** that create areas for inquiry. **Underlying themes** relate ideas, whereas subtle messages emanate from **critical literacy**, which expresses ideas. **Viewpoints** substantiate activities and outcomes. All of these influences on messages merit decoding.

Joint curriculum design assists students and teachers in developing a common focus for courses of study, through collaborative **action research, critical pedagogy,** and **critical literacy** (see Fig. 5.1).

Action Research—Methods of Teaching

Despite state mandates and district guidelines, teachers primarily control course content. They sketch plans and design activities according to the goals and objectives they set. They determine priorities that shape learning experiences. **Joint curriculum design predicates action on a different basis, assuming the importance of student input in the overall course design.**

Joint curriculum design views students as coresearchers who pursue ways to improve learning. They assist in analyzing a course of study in terms of planning, execution, and assessment. The following steps offer one way to begin this process:

1. Develop questions to guide inquiry into methods of teaching and learning that delve into course content.
2. Describe action research—keeping an open mind, sharing impressions, making constructive suggestions.
3. Study regular classroom routines and interactions in light of effectiveness in relation to goals.
4. Establish ways to record student and teacher impressions—anecdotal notes, charts, or checklists.
5. Confer regularly to verify impressions and work toward consensus about how to proceed.

Collecting Data.   Gathering information requires time and patience. Huge amounts of data amass from multiple sources, but rich, thick descriptions from varying vantage points yield patterns of behavior and effect (Merriam, 1990; Strauss, 1990). Identifying these emerging patterns facilitates development of workable concepts suited to particular contexts, or what is known as *grounded theory* (Chenitz & Swanson, 1986).

When Lorraine and Sarah sought change midyear, we planned a semester-long project. During the first 2 weeks, we worked to establish descriptions of the status quo. Lorraine and Sarah wrote professional autobiographies and philosophies of education (see chapter 3). I wrote anecdotal notes, sketched room designs, scripted conversations, charted lesson segments, and taped class sessions. Students completed surveys and wrote responses to open-ended questions.

(Note: I used various instruments that Lorraine and Sarah could have used, if I was not present, by videotaping and reviewing tapes. Replicating specific instruments is not as important as selecting how to gather the information you seek.)

To record specific aspects of teaching and learning, I used a revision of an existing instrument developed by Burns and Anderson (1987). This tool enabled me to chart lesson segments in terms of

(a) purpose, (b) activity format, (c) topic, (d) physical milieu, and (e) teacher and student tasks. Using this schema before any changes began and again after changes had occurred enabled us to see the extent to which joint curriculum design made a difference (see chapter 6). Figure 5.2 shows the main patterns we found.

Data Analysis. Analysis of lesson activity structures revealed strong similarities in all the classes that Lorraine and Sarah taught. Teaching and learning conformed to traditional teacher initiation, student response, and teacher direction or IRE—to a far greater extent than anticipated. Goals and objectives divided content into separate and distinct entities that rarely overlapped. Purposes stressed repetition of material; delivery reflected teacher domination; grouping arrangements and assignment patterns assumed uniformity, as did row and column seating. Despite this overall sameness, teaching personalities and styles differed.

Lorraine stressed students' affective needs. She bolstered students to believe in themselves and their ability to achieve. She attempted to intersperse direct teaching with student learning by doing, but prevailed in tightly managing all activities in attempts to maintain order. Because teaching had become predictable, she sought fresh ideas for herself, as well as for students.

ACTIVITY FORMAT

DELIVERY
- LECTURE
- RECITATION
- DRILL

GROUPING
- WHOLE CLASS
- ROWS AND COLUMNS

ASSIGNMENT PATTERN
- UNIFORM
- REQUIRED
- TIMED

TASK
- TEXTBOOK
- TEACHER DESIGNED
- EXERCISES

DIFFICULTY
- EASY
- LOW LEVEL
- FACTUAL RECALL

INTERACTIONS
- TEACHER - STUDENT

FIG. 5.2. Patterns of teaching *before* applying joint curriculum design.

Sarah felt pressured to cover curriculum. She set goals and designated days for activities that became ritualistic. Memorization reigned over relevance. Sarah rarely drew on her lively intelligence or substantial expertise. Her wealth of knowledge lay idle, along with the prior knowledge students could offer.

Teaching as usual, in both cases, sent clear messages. Preset tasks left little room for inquiry. Strong teacher control and direction left students secondary roles to play. Classroom operations revolved around conformity and factual recall.

What descriptions arise from student notes and your initial assessment of teaching as usual? What messages do actions send regarding teaching and learning?

Overall methods of teaching give general information, but topics and emphases provide more specific signals.

Critical Pedagogy—Topics and Emphases

Critical pedagogy involves examining choices because they define learning experiences. Course outlines schedule topics and reveal emphases. They indicate areas of investigation that send messages regarding key concepts and principles of a subject.

As Lorraine and Sarah described earlier in their own words, district demands held them back from following their dreams. They used required reading lists, writing guides, vocabulary books, and grammar texts. In each class, all students read the same works, wrote formulaic essays, memorized the same vocabulary words, and completed the same grammar exercises. Activities did not vary from section to section or student to student.

Joint curriculum design questions predetermined topics and emphases. Scripts need to be reviewed in order to determine the appeal and efficacy of a play. In like manner, students and teachers need to study course outlines to establish essentials, suggest options, and find areas of common and individual interest. Students and teachers need to be able to associate course concepts with prior frames of reference and move beyond them into new explorations. When probed, knowledge and the quest for knowledge do not stagnate; they thrive. Serious issues of curriculum arise.

What knowledge is valued? Which voices are heard? Are ready answers provided or do students ponder and reflect on material?

Determining Knowledge.   Knowledge is power and for too long people in power decided what was worth knowing and who should be privy to this information (Apple, 1990; Freire, 1991; Giroux, 1994; hooks, 1994). Within the classroom, further distinctions divided those in the know from those silenced or overlooked (Delpit, 1989; Orenstein, 1994; Sadker & Sadker, 1994). Traditional lecturing channeled the flow of information in one direction, from those who enjoyed expert status to unquestioning, passive learners.

Joint curriculum design endeavors to give every learner a clear and audible voice in obtaining, doubting, and scrutinizing knowledge offerings. Information is not automatically accepted or taken for granted, but held up closely to the prism of light that absorbs perspectives and refracts many understandings. Joint curriculum design demystifies knowledge, making it available to all.

Who answers students' questions? Do they expect immediate answers to the information they seek? Do they perform research to discover their own answers?

Personal Understandings.   In our study, Lorraine and Sarah expressed real concerns about dissemination and retention of knowledge. I strongly believe that retention is only as valuable as the extent to which individual learners penetrate information to grasp personal understanding and identify areas for further investigation. These premises guided my observations.

From the anecdotal records I kept during the first weeks of our study, I formed the following impressions.

Lorraine enjoyed class discussions and used a number of techniques to encourage student-initiated comments and questions. Though she wanted to know what students thought, she often foiled her own aims. She elicited student responses by asking leading questions to which only one- and two-word, predetermined answers would suffice. She endeavored to have students elaborate, but rarely encouraged them to interact with each other. Ironically, when permitted to play "teacher," students imitated Lorraine's question-and-answer style, which revolved around factual recall.

Lorraine and I talked about specific examples of when she expected student response, but ended up speaking for students instead. She expressed concern about having students get the right ideas about topics, even though she realized that telling them was not as lasting as allowing them to reach their own conclusions.

In Sarah's case, students followed strict routines. She managed to cover curriculum requirements, but students did not necessarily grasp them or their significance. Students did not express themselves, exchange ideas, or communicate either difficulties or insights. Required to keep notebooks, students mostly recorded isolated lists of answers that lacked context, and therefore meaning.

When we discussed these impressions, Sarah admitted that she exhausted herself by keeping a strict accounting of student completion of every worksheet, class, and homework exercise. Her conscientiousness overpowered her desire to engage students in the joy of learning. She wanted to give students more responsibility, but wondered if they would prove reliable.

For different reasons and in different forms, Lorraine and Sarah sent controlling messages that limited students. Answers had to match preconceived ideas of the teacher or workbook. Willing to please teachers they liked, students were otherwise unmotivated to pursue individual areas of interest related to course topics. Later, with the opportunity to express themselves, they actively sought change.

Joint curriculum design emphasizes the connection of topics and emphases to the type of learning they inspire. Teacher-designed activities may hold little attraction or relevance for students, who get the message that what matters to them is not important to the teacher. Jointly designed activities hold more promise for learners by evoking specific, individualized reasons for pursuing knowledge.

Underlying Themes—Connecting Messages

Themes reveal distinctive qualities that emerge from interactions. They are subtle and materialize over time. Themes connect messages that support actions and ideas. Underlying themes of teaching–learning situations often fail to match intended goals and objectives. Joint curriculum design strives to close the gap for more integrated learning to occur. Joint curriculum design uncovers themes to help learners see connections in course content and inquiry.

To express underlying themes, we used a 25-question survey instrument, the Individualised Classroom Environment Questionnaire or ICEQ (Fraser, 1986), which identified five categories of learning environments akin to key themes or premises of joint curriculum design. **Personalization** enables students to shape learning experiences. **Participation** invites active learning, not passive reception. **Independence** affords choice to pursue information alone or with others. **Investigation** promotes varied student approaches and interests. **Differentiation** permits different levels of learning, as opposed to mastery learning, which expects every student will eventually grasp the same information. The collaborative nature suggested by these themes framed our research.

How would you describe your classes in relation to these categories? How would your students?

Surveying Students and Teachers. Lorraine, Sarah, and their students completed the survey twice—once to describe the actual teaching–learning situation and the second to describe a preferred climate. Results indicated some surprising findings regarding student and teacher perceptions of the person–environment fit (see chapter 4). Predictably, teachers' preconceived notions not only influenced readings of what actually happened, but also swayed expectations for what they could envision.

Lorraine assessed each class differently, reinforcing her belief that students in Period 3 did not participate or initiate investigation as much as those in Period 5. She had felt Period 3 was less interested or academically able and saw the class as less involved. Separately, these students desired far more opportunity for active learning, personalization, and independence than Lorraine hoped for them. In contrast, Period 5, which Lorraine rated as more investigative and independent, scored themselves as less so and did not desire the extent she expected them to seek. Perceptions clearly differed.

On the other hand, Sarah and students from both classes recorded remarkably similar responses to the actual teaching situation, despite very different contexts. Period 2 not only met too early for some students to function well, but also contained students with apparently better self-control than students in Period 7, who came straight from lunch and had difficulty settling down. Differences in class context and composition became subjugated by the prevailing teacher-centered approach. Ironically, agreement among the perceptions of Sarah and her students uncovered sources of Sarah's frustration—she wished students would take a more active part, yet did not design lessons that encouraged them to do so.

In addition, Sarah's dedication to motivating disinterested students drove her to take on the full responsibility for their learning. She wrote:

> Why wasn't I doing what I preferred? I knew the reasons even as I thought of the comparison: number of students, unavailability of books and materials, lack of time to create new freer, looser methods, risk of disorder and administrative unease and blame and castigation.

Sarah questioned her own actions and identified various causes for her dissatisfaction. Students, too, expressed dissatisfaction with the way things were, compared to how they would like them to be. To Sarah's surprise and relief, students desired to be more actively involved in learning than they had been.

Reviewing Surveys. The Friday afternoon that the three of us reviewed student surveys became an exhilarating experience. Lorraine and Sarah felt edified that students appreciated their efforts and concern. At the same time, real student interest in change buoyed them both. Lorraine's classes anticipated change for the better, even though they essentially liked the status quo. Sarah's energetic eighth graders wanted to feel more productive, not just to sit and behave. The ICEQ surveys helped students and teachers compare notes about current and future teaching environments.

Reassured by student interest in change, Lorraine and Sarah turned to student journal entries, summarized below, to garner student concerns and suggestions.

Critical Literacy—Expressing Ideas

Critical literacy acknowledges that wordings suggest multiple levels of meaning. Yet, a series of questions, similar to the ICEQ, directs thinking. To gain further insight into perceptions, we asked students three open-ended questions so they could express themselves in their own words.

Lorraine's classes proffered the following: **What do you like about how this class is run?** "The teacher doesn't rush us to get things done," "the teacher listens to everyone's opinion and we have a chance to discuss them," "reading aloud … I understand more what's going on in the story if it's read aloud," and "the way the teacher breaks everything down to explain what we don't understand."

What has helped you learn? "The teacher," "the class has discussions on things we learn so we go in-depth," "the I's [a district study skill technique used for review and note-taking], and "participating in class."

Overall, both of Lorraine's classes appreciated her interest, concern, and thorough way of teaching. They also did not hesitate to make suggestions for change: **What would you change to help you learn more?** Both classes requested more discussions, group work, voluntary seating arrangements, and more relevant course material. They wanted more individual attention, less textbook work, and more chances to learn from each other.

One amusing difference surfaced—Period 3 wished Lorraine would "lighten up," whereas Period 5 enjoyed her sense of humor. Upon reading these remarks, Lorraine laughed at herself and the realization that she had sobered the scene in Period 3 more than necessary. She admitted to feeling more relaxed with Period 5 because they seemed to grasp content more easily.

Student feedback helped Lorraine realize how she had sometimes unintentionally curtailed learning, causing her to reevaluate her impressions of both classes. She decided to poll students more often for feedback to open the way for constructive change.

Similarly, Sarah's students greatly appreciated her efforts on their behalf. In answer to **What do you like about how this class is run?** and **What has helped you learn?** they cited her drive, organization, understanding, and fairness. They liked and respected her for working hard and being creative in helping them recall facts. However, they also knew quite specifically what they would change for greater ownership in their own learning. They sought more meaning and relevance: **What would you like to change to help you learn more?**

> More classwork and less homework because in class we hardly ever work because we are always checking homework.
>
> One topic at a time because it becomes overwhelming and I can't keep up.
>
> Less repetitious things like reading and doing exercises from the text.
>
> That the teacher not give that many notes but explain it to us better.
>
> The teacher to lecture less, more class discussions, group projects, group activities ... about the real world.
>
> The time of day when we have class until later when I am awake!

Ironically, Sarah's students held similar feelings to hers. They reacted strongly against imposed restraints. They favored greater variety and flexibility in classroom activities. They sought opportunity to work together and learn from each other. Obtaining student feedback helped Sarah to refocus. Mutual dissatisfaction with the way things were proved a solid starting point for change.

Joint curriculum design opens up important lines of communication between teachers and students about issues that otherwise remain unspoken and unaddressed. Dialogue can lead to constructive changes. More importantly, soliciting student feedback sends students the message that what they think really does matter.

Versions—Viewpoints

Joint curriculum design acknowledges that multiple interpretations emerge from patterns of thinking and perceiving, upon which actions and outcomes depend. Outside sources of information add perspective.

In keeping with the strong, active learning component of joint curriculum design, Lorraine and Sarah read professional materials. Written accounts of theories reflected in joint curriculum design not only positioned its philosophy in the literature, but also provided supportive viewpoints. Because cooperative learning, a first stage of joint curriculum design, posed a challenge, they read *Circles of learning* (Johnson, Johnson, Holubec, & Roy, 1984) and *Control theory in the classroom* (Glasser, 1986).

After reading *Circles of Learning*, Lorraine initiated groupwork immediately. From her first attempt, she was struck by the drastic role reversal in the classroom. She was stunned by positive student reaction—in both classes—to becoming more actively involved by having more choice and opportunity for cooperative work.

Her first attempts entailed grouping students to review vocabulary homework exercises, rather than take the entire class through every answer of four exercises. She watched students work more, but worried about the progress of individuals. She felt disconcerted, not feeling in charge of the situation. Lorraine stated:

I felt uncomfortable the first time I grouped for vocabulary to check for the right answers. I asked myself, "Why am I doing this?" ... I've got to get over being nervous about breaking traditional patterns ... I find myself (pause) I don't want them to move, I don't want them to talk.

At the same time, Lorraine began to see potential in joint curriculum design. She expressed curiosity about new forms of assessment, toyed with having students map out their own ideas, and wondered about creativity, structure, and appropriate tasks. She asked about how to explain and apply cooperative learning:

How do you tell them about their roles?
What questions would I give them about a book?
What job would I give each one to do?
If each person represents a character, how do we present it?
How much reading do they have to do to be able to do this?

Joint curriculum design gives students the prerogative: spend time describing and practicing group member roles for shorter tasks, then allow groups to decide who will be responsible for which aspect of investigation, involve students from the beginning of the book, have students generate their own questions, consider group listing or mapping of characters, allow students to decide on modes of presentation.

Lorraine began to envision the difference joint curriculum design made in terms of lesson planning:

I think this whole thing is great. I like this. You learn so much about the book by just bringing in all kinds of ideas. ... You do become desensitized after reading a work a lot.

She gradually realized that her role was changing. Ever concerned with directing events, she began by wanting to dominate, but realized to do so would restrict student participation. Lorraine relied on some of my suggestions at first, but soon allowed students more choice in what *they* would do to accomplish *their* goals.

Joint curriculum design enabled Lorraine to step back from teaching as usual, to see student initiative take hold, to adjust what she had perceived as her need to control, in order for students to be able to accomplish.

Have you experienced similar concerns and doubts? How have you given students more choice? How have students

responded? Have you located professional materials to discuss with students and colleagues?

Sarah took copious notes when reading *Control Theory in the Classroom* (Glasser, 1986). She recognized classroom management as a key element in her teaching. Experience with forceful, unrelenting administrators had trained her to attend to student behavior, almost to a fault. Years of negative criticism about student control had unnerved her. Allowing me to observe all her classes was a major sign of trust. Even then, she was surprised when I only had positive comments at the end of the day, a novel professional experience for her.

Sarah reconsidered the reasons for her classroom decisions. Despite the tremendous amount of thought that had obviously preceded every move, she had focused on control to the detriment of the critical thinking she would have enjoyed and was clearly desirous of encouraging in her students. Opportunities for greater student involvement only took form once Sarah realized she needed to overhaul her approach to teaching.

The importance of flexible physical space, frequent social interaction, and negotiated curricular emphases (see preceding chapters) helped Sarah to redesign lesson plans. She began to recall innovations introduced at conferences in recent years. Past attempts to try these ideas had faltered. With support and guidance, Sarah reveled in the prospect of applying them again and getting feedback on her attempts.

Joint curriculum design renewed Sarah's faith in herself and her students. She stopped feeling that she had to review every single answer, finding more time to do *fun things*. Reading and coaching gave Sarah other viewpoints, which facilitated these changes in teaching.

The process of joint curriculum design gave both teachers and students time to study the messages they were often unconsciously sending to one another. Versions of classroom life began to coalesce as students collaborated with teachers to achieve mutual goals.

MEANINGS

Joint curriculum design alerts students and teachers to the importance of decoding messages to grasp intended and unintended meanings, before being able to experiment with changes. Students and teachers analyze individual performances, methods, and interactions.

Joint curriculum design raises learning to a metacognitive level that requires everyone to be aware of how effective learning occurs. Most teachers plan lessons that fit their preferred learning styles, unconsciously neglecting other approaches. Students generally know how they learn best, but are rarely asked. As the importance of learning styles gains prominence, students and teachers allow for greater choice.

Joint curriculum design assumes that methods determine the meanings students will derive from the teaching–learning situation.

Acceptance of information is not automatic, but open to question, research, and opposition. Learning is not seen as a common experience, but as an individual approach to information. Thus, multiple meanings are derived from messages sent in the learning process.

Individual Performers—Styles of Learning

Teachers and students derive various meanings from the same set of circumstances or ideas. Learning styles affect how learners perceive new information, as much as past knowledge and experiences do.

Traditional teaching assumes all learners are the same. Joint curriculum design does not. Joint curriculum design alerts teachers and students to the differences that characterize learners and the impact that those differences have on the learning process.

What accommodations exist for individual learning styles? How do methods vary to assist students in developing a range of learning styles?

Four categories of learning styles include random, abstract, sequential, and concrete (Gregorc, 1984). Each style represents different ways learners approach new information. As the terms suggest, random or abstract learners tend to be more global than sequential or concrete learners, who prefer orderly, incremental learning. Some learners fit into all categories evenly, others evidence greater emphasis in one or two. No one category is better than another, just different. As a result, the needs of learners differ (Butler, 1984).

One math student teacher described her experience with a tenth-grade geometry class in this manner:

> In the past, I have always enjoyed observing and teaching this class, but today I realized it's going to be harder than I thought. These kids come in after lunch and don't put much effort into answering my questions. They do like doing examples at their seats though. The class seems to be concrete sequential, so I need to change my style of teaching in order to accommodate them.

This student teacher realized the impact of her teaching style on students. She could not continue to teach in accordance with one preferred style if students had trouble following her.

Joint curriculum design honors teachers and students as learners, inviting them to contribute ideas about how to improve learning. This recognition of difference boosts morale and fortifies students and teachers to design varied lessons and learning experiences.

Methods—Models of Teaching

Joint curriculum design invites teachers to employ a wide range of methods that enable more students to derive meaning from learning experiences. Collaboration with students raises awareness of alternatives.

Joyce and Weil's (1995) descriptions of approaches to teaching and learning offer a valuable reference resource of teaching techniques. Strategies like jurisprudential or inquiry learning place students in the center of learning. Synectics sparks creative associations, whereas traditional techniques, like memorization, ground facts. Varied methods offer learners insights into themselves as learners and into the material at hand.

Joint curriculum design does not reserve some information for those in charge, but stresses access to knowledge—about how to learn, as well as what can be learned—so individual performances and interactions gain in quality and meaning.

Multiple Intelligences—Special Talents

Meanings emerge from interactions among performers, as well as from idiosyncratic approaches to learning. Joint curriculum design studies quality of course offerings in terms of interactive learning opportunities.

Students express dissatisfaction and frustration when courses fail to meet their expectations. They speak of not being sufficiently challenged, of having to do seemingly useless and repetitive exercises, or of losing interest because of sheer memorization of facts. Students often fail to see meaning in what they are asked to do.

Joint curriculum design develops interest in schoolwork because interactions are personalized and individualized. Collaboration encourages students to display strengths and apply special talents, which builds self-esteem.

The theory of multiple intelligences identified seven areas of knowledge—logical-mathematical, linguistic, musical, spatial, kinesthetic, interpersonal, and intrapersonal (Gardner, 1991). Traditional schooling relies on the first two, often ignoring the others. Learners who have not excelled in these first two areas have often felt unintelligent. Yet, as research continues, other aspects of knowing, like spirituality, imply still other intelligences (Gardner, 1995). Joint curriculum design invites learners to understand the wide range of knowing and develop many of these intelligences.

When I have shared this theory with students, I have asked them to use it to express understandings of ideas and concepts. Students self-select into the one intelligence they feel is their strongest, though some students fit comfortably in more than one area. Within a class of 25 to 30, students inevitably divide themselves among all seven categories. After 10 to 15 minutes, results are humbling. Students have composed and performed music, written parodies and poetry, developed mathematical equations, or choreographed and performed dance to explain a central point.

Exercises like this awaken students and teachers to the talents that have been hidden in the classroom. To apply this theory of multiple intelligences is to design lessons that allow students and teachers to introduce, process, and express learning in more than paper-and-pencil tests.

Because joint curriculum design stresses student and teacher collaboration throughout the planning process, theories like multiple intelligences arise. With more voice in designing learning experiences, students suggest a range of activities through which to exhibit learning.

SUMMARY

This chapter outlined how to assess regular classroom routines with students, as you begin applying joint curriculum design. First, consider messages inherent in learning situations, then analyze meanings derived from presentation of course content.

Behind-the-Scenes-Mental Preparation: Suggestions for Learning Log Entries

1. Select a colleague to join your study. Arrange for that person to observe your teaching, either in person or through videotaping.

If you have specific areas of interest, list them so your colleague will know to provide specific feedback. If not, leave observations open-ended so you can discuss whatever issues arise. Encourage written feedback so you can review notes at a later date as well.

2. Project ahead into course content you plan to cover. Set a tentative timeline by marking appropriate places in which to start involving students in decision making.

Draw up a tentative schedule for when you will study the usual teaching–learning situation and when you will poll students for feedback and discuss results with them, before beginning the unit in which they will collaborate with you and each other in joint curriculum design.

3. Select professional readings. Enlist a colleague in reading the same material, take notes, and plan time to discuss how concepts match your various teaching contexts.

On-Stage Tryouts: Collaborative Exercises

1. If you chose to do collaborative exercise #3 from chapter 2, direct students to refer to posters of joint curriculum design elements as a means to study regular classroom routines. Suggest they chart what they see, indicate what they like and what they would change, in terms of the elements each student feels are most important.

Consensus: negotiate a timeframe for collecting data.

2. Set aside about 15 to 20 minutes of class time for students to answer open-ended questions like the following:
   a) What do you like about how this class is run?
   b) What has helped you learn?
   c) What would you like to change about the class to help you learn more?

Collect the set of papers, review and discuss results with students.

Consensus: determine key considerations.

3. Elicit from students feedback collected in Activity 1, above. Divide students into small groups to review individual insights and prioritize areas for improvement.

Brainstorm for specific ideas to begin developing options and alternatives to existing practice.

Consensus: Negotiate how to begin implementation.

6

Determining Direction: Developing Emphases

֍ ◆ ֎

Ongoing collaboration with students helps determine direction and develop emphases for specific changes toward an improved teaching–learning situation.

Readings and rehearsals guide a cast of characters to common understandings of a script. Then, actions and interactions among players add nuance. Because context shapes decisions and individual talents color outcomes, interpretations of a play spring from ongoing collaboration.

Interpretations of course content also spring from ongoing collaboration. Choices of topic and emphasis lead classes and sections to different versions of the same basic material. Circumstances and conditions vary from period to period, along with student abilities and talents, altering insights from which conclusions follow.

Joint curriculum design celebrates differences by asking students and teachers to identify strengths within contexts of learning while designing new strategies for learning experiences.

STRENGTHS

Joint curriculum design credits contexts of learning with strengths peculiar to each group of players. Because classes possess individual characteristics, teachers and students act and react differently in each class. Once, traditional approaches complicated learning by treating all teachers and students the same. Joint curriculum design expects differences and frees teachers and students to be themselves in the pursuit of knowledge.

80

What academic, social, and personal characteristics distinguish classes? How are specific strengths applied to negotiate learner participation in determining course direction and roles in each setting?

Learner Abilities

When Lorraine and Sarah first differentiated student abilities, they held higher expectations for one section then they did for the other. As the study progressed, they revised some opinions. Student response indicated that all classes achieved more, given greater freedom of choice. Both the traditionally cooperative classes and more restless classes became more actively involved in learning with joint curriculum design.

A freer and more collaborative climate for learning provided teachers and students with more opportunities to demonstrate strengths. Differences displayed talents, not shortcomings. The following descriptions illustrate changes in views about individual strengths in relation to teaching and learning.

Sarah and Students

Acting on Initial Feedback. Sarah made a dramatic change in plans after we had analyzed feedback in terms of actual and preferred teaching practice (see chapter 5). Originally, she planned the following:

> When we return from the week off, I plan to go over the grammar test, question by question, because nobody will have any books or pencils, no one will be awake, they won't have their heads where they're supposed to be. So this way, I'll provide all the activity. There won't be anything that requires too much effort ... they're supposed to have read *Johnny Tremain*, chapter 2, but I don't think too many of them will have done it.

Instead, Sarah began groupwork immediately and was as surprised as her students to see how quickly they took to it. Students who had done their homework enjoyed peer reading-response writing about *Johnny Tremain*, which released student feelings and opinions about what they had read. Unprepared students felt left out as they sat away from the action quietly reading, trying to catch up with classmates who were clearly enjoying the first signs of joint curriculum design.

This instance exemplified the energy collaboration and trust inspired. Sarah accentuated student strengths and capabilities, instead of assuming the worst. She tactfully allowed unprepared students to save face, rather than receive demerits for not completing the reading assignment. The tenor of class changed from one where rules predominated into a bevy of activity over course content.

Joint curriculum design brought out positive, supportive attitudes. Students evidenced increased interest in learning and Sarah assumed new roles of facilitating progress. She commented on the changes:

> It was strange to have them working and I felt I had nothing to do. ... Now that I don't have to wear myself out going over every question, I can get to all those good stories at the beginning of the book which I never could get to because there's not enough time. I had to give homework, find symbolism, and just ruin it. I think I'm going to read all those good stories just for fun.

Changes in Classwork. Sarah progressed cautiously, demonstrating slow, steady change. Vocabulary workbooks were still being used, but only student-selected problematic examples were discussed. Grammar exercises, though still assigned, were shared and explained in small groups, resulting in more students understanding why certain answers were correct. As traditional means underwent adjustment, students became more active.

At first, Sarah assigned the same task to every group, trying to guarantee that each student learned the same material. As a consequence, group reports became redundant. After we discussed the reality that no two students ever really grasped the same material to the same extent, Sarah varied assignments. The atmosphere became more conducive to personalized, integrated learning, as well as joint efforts.

Encouraged by student response and productivity, Sarah and her students continued to develop and refine group activities. Students mapped out group ideas on poster paper previously reserved for teacher use. They redefined space, sitting on the floor or facing desks together to create workspaces. They focused on content, debating important points, prioritizing, and referring to literary texts to substantiate opinions. They not only read, but reread!

Changes in Students. Joint curriculum design supported Sarah's attempts to change by stressing student input, both spoken and unspoken. As students realized greater responsibility for learning, they took charge of organizing course material and encouraging each other to succeed.

How does independence increase personalization and participation? What new strengths develop?

Sarah noticed that students gained poise before the class. They grasped material more firmly as they explained ideas to each other. They exercised choice and exhibited higher levels of inquiry. No longer waiting for teacher direction, they pursued tasks independently, deciding amongst themselves what to do next and how to do it. They considered Sarah an important resource, but also asked classmates to provide insights to solve problems.

Students concentrated more on the task at hand. No longer forced to conform to restrictive behavior, they relaxed more and eagerly participated. Channeling their energies to increase learning, most students no longer felt the need or desire to disrupt. A few recalcitrants found they could not command as large or willing an audience as before, because purposeful classmates disregarded distracting antics.

Students displayed new attitudes in words as well as actions. I overheard them whisper among themselves: "I like this better ... not so much time is wasted"; "It's not so much like work"; and "It usually took us a whole period to get through this."

Joint curriculum design engendered student enthusiasm, which bolstered Sarah to continue to make changes.

Changes in Lesson Plans. Figure 6.1 offers a composite of the changing classroom lesson activity structures. Compared to the earlier recorded patterns (see Fig. 5.2), definite differences appeared in all areas. Purposes became developmental; delivery switched almost exclusively to being student centered. Uniformity of grouping and assignment patterns disappeared. Difficulty of tasks increased as topics became more integrated and open to interpretation.

Sarah spent her time orienting students, providing feedback, monitoring progress, maintaining the activity flow. Interactive teaching tasks became more productive and personalized, compared to traditional days when she had relegated herself to enforcing class-

ACTIVITY FORMAT

DELIVERY	TASK
DEMONSTRATION	NEGOTIATION
DISCUSSION	COLLABORATION
INQUIRY	STUDENT CHOICE
GROUPING	**DIFFICULTY**
VARIATION	HIGHER LEVEL
FLEXIBLE SETTING	ANALYSIS / SYNTHESIS
	EVALUATION
ASSIGNMENT PATTERN	**INTERACTIONS**
GROUP	STUDENT - STUDENT
INDIVIDUAL	STUDENT - TEACHER
CHOICE	

FIG. 6.1. Lesson activity structures *after* introducing joint curriculum design.

room management rules and disciplining students for restless behavior. Sarah expressed her appreciation for the changes:

> This is exciting and stimulating and satisfying. Summary is boring, I want to know what students think. It's much more fun for me if I can just say to students, 'what did you have problems with?' instead of me putting an 'I' [district study skill technique] on the board and drilling them for factual answers.

Joint curriculum design helped Sarah and her students capitalize on strengths and think on a higher level. She described her experiences:

> I've been doing a lot of directed writing because they have this format we had to follow in the writing guide we've had to use. I would help them. We would organize it together and they'd write the paragraphs. Then we didn't have mistakes in thinking patterns or mistakes in understanding. Now, students make interesting observations. When I did it the old way, we didn't have independent thoughts, inconvenient thoughts.

Expediency is lost when creativity is gained. So, Sarah still struggled with various aspects of joint curriculum design. Relinquishing familiar and predictable teaching patterns did not come easily. Allowing students to proceed at individual rates caused Sarah some concern. Some students, too, complained about having to take on more responsibility for their own learning (see chapter 8).

What difficulties and gains have you encountered? Have you discussed concerns with colleagues and students?

Joint curriculum design encompasses major changes away from traditional teaching. Periods of adjustment differ within contexts of learning, but can draw learners closer together in efforts to achieve. Individual concerns merit airing for group consideration. Mutual understanding provides support mechanisms for changes.

Lorraine and Students

Acting on Feedback. Lorraine gained more confidence in students after she read *Control Theory in the Classroom* (Glasser, 1986) and adapted ideas to fit her needs and those of students. She grouped students for vocabulary activities, spelling reviews, essay writing, and literature analysis. The alacrity with which she made changes attested to the confidence she had in herself and students.

Lorraine found such success and satisfaction with involving students in joint curriculum design that she applied these new measures to all five of her classes! By extending options to all classes, Lorraine discovered additional avenues for learning, as each combination of students developed different ideas. She strengthened her resolve for change.

I had anticipated this would happen, but not so soon. Past experience with implementing joint curriculum design invariably followed the same path. The benefits of joint curriculum design had always proven worthwhile for teachers and students of all grade levels and abilities.

Have you extended joint curriculum design to all classes? To what extent do students collaborate?

Changes in Attitude. Lorraine's actions changed markedly. She circulated around the room, noting where experimentation was working well and where she needed to provide extra support. She felt secure enough to consult with me briefly during class for suggestions on refinements.

Joint curriculum design created a positive sense of what students could accomplish, early in implementation. Advantages were quite obvious, but roots of change need time to grow, so reservations still surfaced. At one point, Lorraine claimed, "I give advanced classes more cooperative work, because they can be trusted." She still held on to original distinctions in perceptions of what different classes could accomplish, even though all classes were demonstrating more capability than she had originally believed they possessed.

Lorraine noted more students had been working than when she had conducted class along strictly traditional lines. Yet, students who resisted the idea of working harder worried her. She mused, "We've been programmed to feel that every child has to get everything out of every lesson." She then added:

> The ones who don't like it are the ones who never did any work, but now they're forced into a situation where they can't get away with it because it's obvious to everyone.

Lorraine weighed the differences that emerged. Initial concern for individual students lessened as they, too, became involved. Slower students accomplished more in the freer atmosphere in which work was discussed, instead of "covered" at a pace they had not been able to keep up. Less inclined students responded to peer pressure to succeed much faster than they did to rules or authority figures. Joint curriculum design encouraged all individuals to show what they could contribute.

Have students resisted changes? Have you intervened or allowed peers or more time to influence adjustment?

Changes in Actions. Lorraine's questioning became more open-ended. She spent more time eliciting student response and less time trying to get students to guess her meaning. She felt less constrained to check every stage with every group. She designed tasks that required student collaboration to arrive at answers.

For example, she assigned students to groups to write creative pieces, using vocabulary words from a common list. Circulating among groups, Lorraine overheard a variety of approaches to accomplishing the task. Some students defined words first, decided which words to use, then methodically tried to apply them in a set order. Others checked meanings together, but decided to write individual creative stories. Still others worked in round robin fashion, each group member supplying a sentence containing a vocabulary word. Lorraine enjoyed the novelty that joint curriculum design encouraged.

When a single method is required of all students, some students have difficulty following the method although they could handle the material. Thus, forced to follow a structure foreign to their style of thinking, some students fail at tasks despite their ability to grasp content.

Have learning styles been introduced? Are students encouraged to develop different learning styles?

Joint curriculum design helped Lorraine to remember that alternate approaches broaden access to knowledge. Practice enabled students to discover unique paths to reach common goals.

Changes in Lessons. Figure 6.2 reveals the extent to which classroom activity structures changed during implementation.

Lorraine shifted away from teacher-centered approaches toward jointly directed learning. Class groupings and assignment patterns changed frequently. No more were days routinely predictable. Delivery developed into new possibilities, like student reporting. As a result, interactions between Lorraine and her students became more personalized and individual. Students designed activity formats and joint purposes.

Content switched from isolated skill drills to integrated and meaningful tasks. Grammar evolved from writing. Writing developed out of the exploration of literature. Vocabulary, though still taken from prescribed lists in vocabulary books, became entwined with creative writing. Spelling partners helped each other attend more to precision. Task authenticity increased student motivation and interest in learning. Students investigated ideas and concepts.

Joint curriculum design stressed individual accountability, causing learners to take action and freeing Lorraine to provide individual attention to students in need of assistance.

Innovations. Joint curriculum design also invited innovation. For the first time in her long career, Lorraine taught two major works of literature simultaneously, by having each half of the class responsible for one of these titles. The chairperson had expected her to teach both novels in four weeks. She knew students didn't read much and would never complete both works in that period of time.

ACTIVITY FORMAT

DELIVERY

LECTURE	DEMONSTRATION
RECITATION	DISCUSSION
DRILL	INQUIRY

GROUPING

WHOLE CLASS	VARIATION
ROWS AND COLUMNS	FLEXIBLE SETTING

ASSIGNMENT PATTERN

UNIFORM	GROUP
REQUIRED	INDIVIDUAL
TIMED	CHOICE

TASK

TEXTBOOK	NEGOTIATION
TEACHER DESIGNED	COLLABORATION
EXERCISES	STUDENT CHOICE

DIFFICULTY

EASY	HIGHER LEVEL
LOW LEVEL	ANALYSIS / SYNTHESIS
FACTUAL RECALL	EVALUATION

INTERACTIONS

TEACHER - STUDENT	STUDENT - STUDENT
	STUDENT - TEACHER

FIG. 6.2. Comparison of activity structures *before* and *after* implementing joint curriculum design.

We discussed trying something new—divide the reading assignment to give students ample time to read one complete novel. Though student choice would be more in keeping with the negotiation inherent in joint curriculum design, Lorraine felt compelled to assign books according to student reading levels. Students liked the novelty of splitting the work and accepted whichever book they received without protest. Ultimately, the goal would encompass clear student choice, but it takes time to reach that point.

Lorraine proceeded to teach a mini-lesson on theme or characterization and then divide students into two groups to identify parallels in the books they were reading. Solid results pleased her and empowered students. Students offered and defended differing interpretations, raising the level of critical thinking considerably. They negotiated within groups, which honed speaking skills. Students identified themes and symbols that Lorraine had not considered in all the years she had taught those works. She realized how she had unwittingly restricted student thinking in the past.

Joint curriculum design allowed time for students to consider material rather than breeze past it. Students wanted to do a good job and enjoyed success. Classmates began to question each other about the other book, comparing plots, characters, symbols, and themes. Through this exchange of ideas, each group gained a clearer understanding of the elements of literature. The finale was the best. Some students actually asked for permission to read both books! The inductive philosophy of joint curriculum design had lured students into wanting to learn more.

These two narratives suggest the extent to which Sarah and Lorraine developed understandings of the philosophy behind joint curriculum design by implementing various elements. They drew on strengths, but students mostly noticed changes in strategies.

STRATEGIES

Schools of acting train players for the stage. They all deal with similar aspects of the trade and art, but each school has specialty areas. Students choose schools of acting for those distinguishing features that will help them perform more convincingly.

Public school students generally lack that wonderful element of choice. Despite some movement toward charter schools or vouchers, most students attend school in their geographical district and acquiesce to a schedule of teachers and courses prepared by others.

Joint curriculum design challenges every teacher to create a collaborative climate for learning that students would choose if they had the chance. The key to achieving this status is a repertoire of strategies.

What strategies improve learning? What comments and feedback do students receive and provide?

Reactions to change vary from one individual to another. Strategies that ease learning for one student do not necessarily have the same effect on all. For this reason, students provide frequent, specific feedback throughout implementation of joint curriculum design.

Sarah and Students

Adjusting to Change.   Initially, Sarah felt "weird" because she had expended less energy while students had worked nonstop for whole class periods. Students gave opinions more freely and attained higher levels of critical thinking. Period 7 amazed her, outshining the class originally described as more cooperative. Students had come to class better prepared and more willing to participate. Even formerly unruly students chimed in constructively.

Unable to contain her excitement, Sarah began to attend weekly informal gatherings in the principal's office to share her experiences of developing joint curriculum design. She wanted to stimulate colleagues to reconsider how they taught and join her in improving the teaching–learning situation for them and their students.

Sarah worked at becoming more flexible to grant students leeway, but she also reported:

> I would have given up on this weeks ago if you weren't here coaching me because I would have come up against some of these problems; I would have looked around and said to myself, 'Well, the chairperson is looking over my shoulder, there's too much noise in here … we'll go back to the old way.

Because joint curriculum design is so comprehensive, teachers can lose heart, despite personal rewards and positive student responses. For this reason, I believe that consulting with at least one colleague alleviates some stress associated with change and unknown consequences. Colleagues provide outside perspectives of how classroom climates and learning experiences become more personalized and students become more energized.

Sarah wavered for about a month. Students were reading, participating, being responsible. She was overjoyed with their interest and spontaneity. However, she began to redirect her old habits of policing behavior into strictly recording every student effort as extra credit. Accounting was weighing her down again. Such record keeping seemed unnecessary and counterproductive. Students had been working harder, learning more. Test grades evidenced improvement (see chapter 9). Students enjoyed learning for learning's sake.

Persistence paid off for Sarah. Concerns about noise levels and student participation had existed in former traditional settings as well. The difference with joint curriculum design was that noise and activity marked constructive learning. The entire atmosphere had changed from dominance to dialogue. Student success convinced her that changes had enhanced learning.

Student Perceptions of Change. Students reacted strongly to the changes. In journals, they answered more open-ended questions.

What was different about this class? How did your job change? What did you like? What didn't you like?

Representative replies from students in Period 2 include:

The teacher obviously paid attention to all our requests … instead of reading answers out of the book, she asked us which one we had trouble with. We did mapping which was fun. We all worked together which was an interesting experience. I feel that when we get in groups and when the teacher shows interest in the class, I think the class would respond the same way.

Everything went a lot smoother this week in my opinion. I think that it wasn't as hectic and we had more discussions. I got a new seat. I was more into the class. Because things are more active, I think people get more active in things, when they're having fun.

Representative comments from Period 7 include:

The teacher communicates more to us in a good way … the teacher seems to trust us more. I was more aware of what was happening and I was more interested. I also felt I should make-up my homework, which I did.

Everyone wasn't as bored and I think everyone enjoyed doing things differently. We didn't all get bored and start talking as much because we were busy with something that occupied our time.

These positive comments reassured Sarah that students preferred the new strategies. She put into perspective the complaints from a few students who preferred going over every workbook answer. She surmised that these few students split into one of two categories—those who never did homework and relied on lists of answers to fill in the blanks or those who performed well but worried about making mistakes.

Joint curriculum design incurred trade-offs. Sarah felt the majority of students enjoyed benefits she would not suspend for the sake of a few. Most strategies brought out positive learning experiences.

What new strategies have developed in your classes? How have students responded to these new strategies? Have students suggested new strategies as well?

Lorraine and Students

Building Trust.   Lorraine had actively wanted change and particularly liked the coaching aspect, which offered immediate feedback and alternatives. Consulting with colleagues raises the level of investment and success. Lorraine assessed the change in students, commenting, "They're asking such good questions." Collaboration encouraged her to take risks she never had before.

One major concern Lorraine voiced involved student lack of interest in reading: classtime explanations of assigned chapters had been so thorough that students had little incentive to go back to read on their own, if they had not already done so. We talked about giving students permission to pick up where the last class discussion had left off. Lorraine tried this realistic strategy and reported, "I told my tenth graders if they haven't kept up with the reading of a book, just jump in and I think some of them did." Although reading only part of a book pales in comparison to reading the entire work, this strategy accomplished Lorraine's goal of getting more students interested in reading.

Lorraine's students answered questions after changes had begun. Representative answers follow.

What changes have occurred in this classroom?

Period 3 students wrote:

Whatever assignments we are doing, we do together. ... We have more writing assignments than usual. I like the idea that we do vocabulary together as a group and then check it over.

The atmosphere has been more relaxed.

Our tasks are more independent.

Period 5 students wrote:

We had to get together and get along with our classmates. I learned much easier in groups.

She's giving us the opportunity to communicate better with our fellow peers.

Instead of just sitting there and letting the teacher tell us the answers, we got to pick groups and work amongst ourselves.

I realized my grades are getting better.

Students not only felt they had gotten to know each other and course content better, but that they had also learned how to work together to accomplish goals. They expressed awareness of improved communication, as well as heightened interpersonal responsibility.

Domains of Learning.   As explained in preceding chapters, joint curriculum design promotes growth in all three domains of learning—cognitive, social, and affective. Though students were unaware of these domains per se, they clearly recognized benefits in all three areas.

How did your job change?

Period 3 students answered:

My job was easier. I didn't have to do as much work.

It feels like the teacher is trying to make us have fun so we have actually worked more.

I had to work very hard and think more.

I don't have to be the only one thinking of ideas, I just ask the people I'm working with.

Usually I have great difficulties, but ever since the class has been doing groupwork, it's been very easy.

Period 5 students answered:

I had to put some of my ideas in the group that I worked with to show that I wasn't sitting back and letting everyone else do the essays or vocabulary.

I didn't have to do the work alone and if I did, we would compare answers and correct wrong ones.

What I had to do different was talk more and learn to work in groups.

We didn't have to do as much work because the assignment was divided among three or four people. So it's easier and more fun to do the work.

I started to have more input.

I had to do my vocabulary much more carefully than I used to. Also I had to get along with people in my groups. I also had to learn how to stand in front of the room.

Joint curriculum design caused significant changes. Students viewed classwork as being more manageable and accessible with the aid of classmates. They felt they worked less, but gained more. Differences in approach had caused far more personal accountability, a change students acknowledged and appreciated.

Did you like the changes? Why or why not?

Period 3 students responded:

You get to hear what other people have to say.

I like the changes because we work with our friends and it gives us a chance to think.

I get to work and help others, and they also help me, too.

I like the changes because if one person doesn't know it, the other person could help you with the problem.

Period 5 students responded:

I am learning more than I used to. I have also realized that I am having fun while doing it. The time is going faster.

Yes. We find out what everybody thinks is the right answer and how to answer the question the best way.

You really get to know the kids in your class better.

More freedom to do things and we get to interact.

These responses indicated student enthusiasm for the difference joint curriculum design makes in terms of thinking at more challenging levels. They also revealed benefits of knowing classmates' interests, personalities, and intellectual capacities.

What specific changes would you like to see happen?

Students suggested the following: "More group work with friends," "Let students teach class," "Keep moving on without staying on a topic too much," "See our work be dramatized more by movies, film, class trips." Also, "More class discussions/debates because I learn better that way," "Assigned groups that we work with all the time," "Groups to study together and make tests together and get the same grade," and "Act out what we read."

Students had clear ideas about how to continue to improve conditions for learning. Just a few weeks of joint curriculum design had alerted them to possibilities for more active learning and decision making.

Perhaps the most remarkable fact about all of the student journal entries was their unanimity. Not one student complained about the changes. They all enjoyed joint curriculum design and requested more freedom to learn interactively. They recognized and appreciated the effort it took to work cooperatively, but clearly valued the benefits. They adjusted quickly and well.

How have students accepted changes? Have they requested additional changes?

Open lines of communication remind students that their input is essential to the success of joint curriculum design. Students recognize the metacognitive nature of identifying and applying how they learn best in various learning experiences.

Student Work Samples. Student work samples attested further to the extent to which students adapted to joint curriculum design.

Work improved. Students wrote peer reading-response journals, in which they expressed feelings and opinions of storylines to which other classmates wrote replies. They considered the destructive consequences of greed, believability of characters and events, the relevance of actions and plots to their own lives (Gross, 1992b).

Student analysis of main and secondary characters, symbolism, and themes for books they were reading revealed a more sophisticated awareness of comparison and cause and effect than Lorraine had witnessed previously in her teaching career. She felt these students truly understood distinctions and articulated them better than students had been able to do in the past (Gross, 1991).

Joint curriculum design introduced students and teachers to co-operative learning strategies. Sarah and Lorraine maintained more control over course content and methods than the flexible balance among teachers and students that joint curriculum design entails. However, as they gained competence in cooperative ventures, they moved toward more collaborative decision making with students, showing a higher level of trust and confidence.

SUMMARY

This chapter described how joint curriculum design builds on the strengths of students and teachers as players in different contexts of learning. With help from observers, changes in specific strategies result in enhanced learning situations.

Behind-the-Scenes Mental Preparation:
Suggestions for Learning Log Entries.

1. Enumerate the strengths you see in each class with which you work. List how you identify these strengths and how you encourage students to build on them.

How else could you learn about students' strengths?

2. State what teaching strategies you have changed in order to implement joint curriculum design. Note specific results. State which strategies you have added as you became more involved in joint curriculum design. List specific results.

Compare the two descriptions to find the strengths of your teaching that have facilitated change.

3. Share your descriptions with one or more colleagues to discuss how teaching and learning have improved and how additional changes may further benefit you and students.

On-Stage Tryouts:
Collaborative Exercises for Implementation

1. Ask students to list five strengths they possess. After at least 5 minutes, instruct them to list five more strengths. This really

challenges some, but brainstorming generally produces better answers among the later ideas.

Pair students to discuss the difficulty they had in recognizing their abilities. Encourage them to share specific answers with one another and provide examples to each other of instances where they have seen those attributes in action.

2. Ask students to keep a running list of curricular changes they feel have helped them learn more. Encourage them to be specific. At reasonable intervals, invite class discussions about student progress or concerns and cull suggestions for other innovations that could be tried.

3. Depending on the number of students in a class, divide the class into four or five groups, assigning one person in each as leader, observer, clarifier, recorder, and reporter. (The last two roles may be combined).

Ask each group to review a homework assignment or ongoing project, maintaining assigned group roles.

Jigsaw groups by role to allow leaders, observers, clarifiers, recorders, or reporters to discuss their impressions and formulate role definitions. They may map ideas on poster paper or the blackboard.

Employ large-group discussions to exchange experiences that will further understanding of group dynamics to accomplish tasks.

7

Checking Props:
Researching Resources

❀ ◆ ❁

Reconsider the known and familiar in the teaching–learning exchange. **Joint curriculum design** stresses creative use of space, realia, and resources.

Stage craft builds a set. Scene changes and stage props assist actors, just as decisions about space and provisioning assist teachers and students in building an environment for learning.

No public school classroom ever has enough room or resources. Every teacher has an ongoing wish list and many spend large sums of money from personal funds to provide more for students. Some schools, as Kozol (1991) described in *Savage Inequalities*, lack bare necessities, whereas others race to keep up with state-of-the-art technology. Great disparities exist.

Major reforms of financial backing for public education strive to provide more equitable access to knowledge. Government, corporate, and university efforts create partnerships with schools to expand resources.

Joint curriculum design recognizes the potential in exploration and expansion of human and material resources to enrich learning. Figure 7.1 suggests dimensions of a learning context that are often neglected or underused.

STAGE SETTING: MATERIAL RESOURCES

Set "designers work in the theater creating the scenery, costumes, sound and lighting so necessary for a play to come to life" (Smiley,

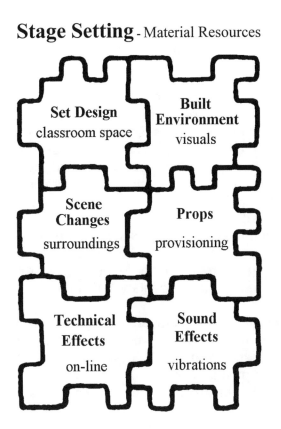

Stage Setting - Material Resources

Set Design classroom space	**Built Environment** visuals
Scene Changes surroundings	**Props** provisioning
Technical Effects on-line	**Sound Effects** vibrations

FIG. 7.1. Joint curriculum design stresses use of resources that support active learning.

1987, p. 119). Teachers, too, select ideas, objects, and situations to inject life into learning. Novelty aids students in constructing knowledge. Creative choices make the familiar, strange, and the strange, familiar.

Set Design—Classroom Space

As set designs transform a standard theater stage, use of classroom space either cramps or extends learning experiences. Joint curriculum design involves studying surroundings to insure that physical forces encourage, rather than discourage, active learning.

What classroom features are fixed? What features are flexible? What specific changes would invite new learning experiences?

Fixed Features.   At first glance, the fixed nature of a room seems to preclude certain kinds of teaching and learning, but careful reassessment can change what seems unalterable.

One student teacher I supervised in an urban setting taught a class of 35 in a small, crowded room with a raised platform in the front. To open space, she converted the platform into a stage from which students performed skits and readings, sprawled out to work in groups, or settled down for sustained silent reading.

Fixed theater seating poses problems for interactive learning to happen. Seats may be immovable, but students are not. I have asked students to wriggle around in their seats to form groups with those nearby rather than remain sedentary and out of one another's view.

Flexible Features.   To disregard the fact that some features are flexible causes them to appear fixed, yet rearranging movable items (other than desks, which are discussed in chapter 4) stimulates a welcoming and productive climate.

Location and function of furniture signal pathways and cue players about how they are expected to move. Loughlin and Suina (1982) studied classrooms to improve learning contexts. Their practical suggestions included availability of student workspaces and storage areas.

Who uses file cabinets or bookcases and how? Does the largest desk in the room serve only one purpose? What access do students have?

Bulky file cabinets can obstruct vision and movement, or be positioned to create a quiet corner for independent study. They can inconveniently line a wall, or be catty-cornered to break a rigid look to a room and become more accessible. How functional are file cabinets? Are vertical files current? Is there room for storage of student work, especially in these days of individual portfolio development?

Built-in closets or bookcases may also be put to better use. Some hold class sets of reference materials, like dictionaries, whereas others stock outmoded textbooks. Taking inventory and discarding extraneous items can clear the way for more versatile resources.

A teacher's desk often serves as temporary or short-term storage. By moving reference materials to shelves or tops of file cabinets, I have uncovered advantages to providing a large clear surface. Bigger students have found comfort working in an area more suited to their size; groups have gathered around a common workspace.

One teacher with whom I worked replaced student desks with large tables. One table accommodated two to four students, where individual desks had cluttered the room before. Seating supported cooperative learning.

Joint curriculum design values brainstorming options with students. If you canvass school storage areas, alternative furnishings might be closer than you think.

Built Environments—Visuals

Within a built environment, students and teachers react—not only among themselves, but also to objects around them (Barker, 1968). Open classrooms of the 1960s and 1970s went to extremes of removing walls to enlarge learning space. Premises governing this strategy included the desire to provide a rich environment to promote innate curiosity and exploration (Barth, 1972). "Open spaces, open groups, open activities, open education, open-ended education" (Bremer & Bremer, 1972, p. 131) promised learners independence.

For secondary students, open classrooms shifted learning from "standard operations tied to specific contexts," to "exploration of principles ... in a context of self-discovery" (Bernstein, 1975, p. 70). Recent studies in cognition have reinforced these assumptions about learning (Glaser, 1990; Walberg, 1990), but have left walls intact! Similar goals drive the math, social studies, and English standards of the 1990s. Joint curriculum design encourages built environments.

Display Facilities. Besides developing workspaces and storage areas, Loughlin and Suina (1982) stressed display facilities. Bulletin boards and blank walls provide huge surfaces for creative redefinition.

What displays fill the classroom? Do bulletin boards and wallspace extend learning? Do students contribute?

When I first began teaching, I searched for materials to brighten the classroom and provoke student thought. Travel posters and large, calendar photographs became springboards for creative writing. Magazine covers or newspaper headlines prompted expository essays. Decorations supported activities. When students offered to arrange bulletin boards, I found the limits of my artistry. Displays became class responsibilities. Month to month, original designs, based on course content, lent a warmth and glow to the room. Soon, student work covered wallspace as well.

Lorraine and Sarah arranged bright, cheerful rooms. Window plants thrived and written student work and quotes from key authors filled bulletin boards. However, as class activities changed, so did decorations. Photos of group skits and presentations personalized decor for students, as did student artwork inspired by individual and group work.

Furthermore, the entire classroom can excite learner curiosity, as ceiling lights and fixtures offer three-dimensional display space. Sensory perceptions sharpen in math rooms where geometric designs swing from above, science rooms where chemical compound mock-ups sway overhead, and social studies or foreign language rooms where cultural artifacts fill the air.

Joint curriculum design invites a lively, informative learning environment, to avoid dead space and capture the essence of a course through student graphics.

Beyond the Classroom. To reach beyond the classroom is to extend the radius of space. Windows let in air, light, and the outside world. For years, my classroom overlooked a football field and thoroughbred exercise track across the street. When students weren't looking out the windows, I was. Band practices or thrown jockeys, lightning storms or bees from the track rosebushes caught our attention. Weaving unexpected sights and sounds into lessons, we managed the real world to perform for us.

The busier the neighborhood, the more varied the scenery. My son taught on the seventh floor where windows faced the downtown section of a large city. Jet planes and skylines, sirens and billboards, subways and smokestacks sparked student imaginations, as did movie-making scenes shot in the street below. Weaving these signs and symbols into class animated schooling.

Scene Changes—Alternative Surroundings

Joint curriculum design unleashes learning from one stationary setting. Media or lab rooms offer experiences ordinary classrooms can't match. Cafeterias and auditoriums, stairwells and corridors afford unconventional perspectives. Unused and seemingly unlikely areas await detection.

A lover of the outdoors, I've never found enough air indoors. Whenever possible, I take classes outside. So do my students. One physics student teacher had classes climb field grandstands to conduct gravity experiments, another brought classes to a hill adjacent to the school to solve problems of force and motion.

As always, field trips expose students to information and experiences on a first-hand basis. Rural students rarely explore the cultural offerings of the nearest major city; urban students rarely commune with nature. Students relish such changes of scenery.

Props—Provisioning

Props lend an aura of reality to set designs as realia ground examples for learning. What wonderful irony behind the term *realia*. To think that such a word would even exist in our lexicon. Have schools been so remote from living that a term had to be coined to suggest using actual objects as tools for teaching?

Realia. Authenticity and the lasting validity of learning from hands-on experiences has long been documented (Dewey, 1899). Yet, few teachers act on this information by bringing realia into the teaching–learning situation. Secondary level teachers, especially, resist what they think of as elementary school trimmings or trappings. Unfortunately, this attitude disadvantages everyone. Visual and tactile learners lose out if hands-on learning opportunities are rare or nonexistent; logical-rational learners lose the chance to develop visual and tactile capacities (Gardner, 1995).

Realia reinforce associative thinking. For example, I have distributed *Monopoly* play money to elicit student memories of winning and losing, before using different denominations to discuss privilege and discrimination. Visuals reinforced abstract concepts.

What resources exist in the classroom? What articles can be added? How have students contributed resources?

Gathering Resources. Provisioning stimulates learner curiosity; gathering materials need not be expensive. Joint efforts can result in collecting recent issues of newspapers or magazines from home or neighbors. Library discard sales and used book stores can supply classroom lending libraries and reference resources.

Lorraine and Sarah applied for a district minigrant to stock class-rooms with paperback books dealing with teenage and multicultural issues. They developed units of study in which students selected issues, read related works, and presented group projects. Proactive, both teachers upgraded available resources and gave students the chance to research social concerns, identify hotline resources, and inform one another of outreach programs.

A colorful array of items can amass in a classroom if students are encouraged to bring in realia. One tenth-grade class chose hats to portray settings for a short story unit, evoking images of beachfronts and fiestas, train yards and sporting arenas, as groups role played skits of storylines. Similarly, a ninth-grade class sought everyday objects that revealed cultural heritage. They wrote original myths about things like candles as objects that mark birthdays and religious celebrations.

Later, recycling items expanded learning by creating new asso-ciations through comparisons or contrasts. Hats prompted students to explore characterizations; candles lit darkened rooms to simulate city life during a blackout. Realia formed frameworks to organize ideas.

Specific items leave lasting impressions. A student teacher of Spanish passed around photographs of her year abroad. Snapshots of bullfights, processions, and dances piqued student interest. In her learning log, she noted "they enjoyed seeing things firsthand. They had plenty of questions and wanted to hear music from Sevilla."

A math student teacher brought in copies of local supermarket fliers for a Consumer Math class to develop grocery lists based on proposed weekly food budgets. A second math student teacher brought in Internal Revenue Service forms to help students file income tax returns.

Joint curriculum design engaged students and teachers in search-ing everyday life for connections with course content to reinforce relevance.

Technical Effects—On-Line

Technical effects electrify learning. Television and audio and video recorders turned on push-button, video-age students long before personal computers and CD-ROMs. From video games to music videos, students spend most waking hours wired in some way. Computers claim whole generations of young, active minds because a computer culture defines much of their lives. Youth take to the screen to such an extreme that they often forego fresh air and exercise.

Joint curriculum design embraces technology. Rather than try to compete with the blips, beeps, and dazzle of electronic equipment, teachers work with students to bring the information age into the classroom.

Distance Learning.   Joint curriculum design encourages interactive and distance learning to reach beyond the known. Internet, television, and phone connections broaden access to knowledge. Internet services offer new ways to collect data and disseminate information through the World Wide Web and discussion groups. Telepresences and immersions place learners into simulations and synthetic worlds of virtual realities. Interconnections proliferate daily.

Mind-boggling speed of technological advances daunts even the wealthiest districts that strive to keep up with state-of-the-art facilities. To achieve access or the ability to update ineffectual technology requires funding, planning, and ongoing retooling. As new technologies continue to pervade the working world, school districts must wire buildings, train staff, and expose students to on-line learning (O'Neil, 1995). Classroom initiatives can hurry the process.

Vision, drive, and tenacity convert new modes of transmitting information into new approaches to constructing knowledge. Rather than mimic texts and images available through other sources, joint curriculum design spurs teachers and students to create ways to contact and interact with learners and primary sources across the nation and beyond.

What connections link students with technology? What other modes could be investigated and developed? How do students exhibit skills?

Technological Expertise.   Students often have a better sense of the computer world than teachers. Challenge them to design lessons that apply technological skills in the pursuit of knowledge. Design research projects to link students with other sites. Immediacy improves motivation. My classes waited weeks for responses from international penpals before e-mail shrunk waiting time considerably. Bring teleconferences into the classroom or bring students to a local library or public building that can provide such an opportunity. Given the chance to explore electronic pathways, students exhibit more personal responsibility for learning and rely less on teachers for information (Mehlinger, 1996).

Where districts and homes share computer access, school–home partnerships reinforce layers of learning. Families keep abreast of homework assignments and school events or share areas of expertise at the click of a mouse. Education never resided solely in the schools. Developing ways to hook up homes and schools revives the interdependent nature of influences on students' lives.

Joint curriculum design encourages teachers and students to plug in and stay on line.

Sound Effects—Vibrations

Sounds carry meanings. The number and timbre of voices tell a tale. A single voice lacks the vibrancy and range a chorus can reach. Sounds also indicate kinds of learning and levels of student engagement.

What voices fill the classroom? Is everyone heard on a regular basis? Are diverse views and opinions welcome?

One math student teacher observed a veteran teacher:

> Although he's nice, his teaching needs a little work. He speaks too fast when teaching and sometimes rambles, he singles out students who have high achievements—how do the rest of the students feel?—and he doesn't allow the students to do all of the work—he cuts them off or does it for them, saying 'there's no need to do these if you haven't done them since I'm giving you the answer.'

This student teacher recognized the value of individual input and esteem. She wondered how this teacher knew what students actually learned, because he relied so heavily on telling them, rather than eliciting from them the level of comprehension. She questioned why he did not offer students the chance to complete examples to experience success or learn from mistakes.

In contrast, joint curriculum design honors individual voice and prompts original thought. Interactive learning charges the air with the sounds of expressive voices. Lilting questions pose problems;

thoughtful silences engender the hum of discussions; spirited exclamations accompany "aha" moments.

Joint curriculum design raises the decibel level of learning. Enthusiastic voices, the natural extension of dialogue and discovery, replace the lull of a single voice. Lorraine took time to get used to the change:

> I don't need quiet all the time—do you think the other teachers mind the noise? ... I was going to ask the chairperson if the noise bothered him, but I decided not to because it's constructive, it's always under control, and I can get them back.

When we discussed this concern, Lorraine realized she was projecting her own reservations. When students spoke up in class, she found it difficult to keep silent. She felt pressured by the need to listen to students speaking in different groups. With practice, she learned to circulate, comment where appropriate, and adjust to the heightened sound effects of learning.

Sarah welcomed student involvement, but knew her own tolerance level for noise, no matter how constructive. She devised an accommodation to deal with the buzz and babble of voices. She chose to wear ear plugs rather than squelch new found student enthusiasm for learning.

Besides the liveliness that joint curriculum design inspires, questioning changes. Students learn to speak their minds. It is refreshing to hear what students actually think when they feel free to probe deeper.

Joint curriculum design offers learners genuine give-and-take, reciprocal opportunity to be heard. Diverse opinions provoke thought. Openly invited to express connections, students enjoy spontaneity and imagination. Whimsy leads to invention more often than not.

THEATER COMMUNITY: HUMAN RESOURCES

No theater production is a solo act. Even the writer who chooses to produce, direct, and star in his or her own work relies on others to bring that dream to fruition. The theater community offers helping hands.

Theater Community - Human Resources

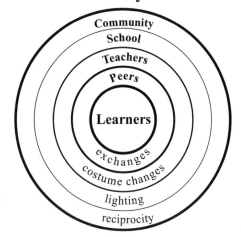

FIG. 7.2. Circles of human resources that influence and contribute to joint curriculum design.

Joint curriculum design presumes community as the base for interactive and integrated learning. Class investigations are collaborations that reach beyond the class and school building, into the community (see Fig. 7.2).

How is community defined? What forms of outreach exist? How do families and local or global community members contribute to student learning?

Learners—Personalized Input

Each learner possesses a wealth of prior knowledge from which the entire class can benefit. Each learner employs unique learning styles by which to approach, construct, and express knowledge. Yet, the immeasurable resource each student represents is ignored in classrooms that fail to ignite student interest and response.

Greene (1971) argued that "we pay too little attention to the individual in quest of his own future" (p. 253). She outlined restraints that held students back and described ways to unfetter and empower learners. Imagine public education enacted under her vision:

> New syntheses within experience … awareness of the process of knowing, of believing, of perceiving … opens up the possibility of presenting curriculum in such a way that it does not impose or enforce … the student is enabled

to recognize that reason and order may represent the culminating step in his constitution of a world ... to generate the structures of the disciplines on his own initiative ... he may realize that he is projecting beyond his present horizons each time he shifts his attention and takes another perspective on his world. (p. 268)

Joint curriculum design strives to give students such breadth of experience in which to examine ideas, explore hunches and hypotheses, and draw tentative conclusions.

Personalization of education builds on prior knowledge and nurtures self-regulatory skills and interpersonal interaction (Bruner, 1966; Glaser, 1990; Keefe, 1989; Walberg, 1990). Self-directed learning and collaboration prod teachers and students to continually learn about themselves, each other, and the curriculum.

Teachers who offer personalized education operate in a learning environment that balances "the learner's knowledge, processing strategies, concepts, learning sets, motivational systems, and acquired skills" (Keefe, 1989, p. 74). They worry less about covering content and concentrate more on developing strategies that appeal to a cross section of students.

Progressives have always focused on learners to counteract isolation from reality and encourage the growth of imagination. Kilpatrick (1925) felt learning began in the earliest stages of exploration, so he fostered learner control of purpose, plan, execution, and judgment. Assumptions behind this thinking encompassed the importance of who the learner was and how the learner chose to acquire knowledge. One spin-off of the *project method* was Foxfire (Wigginton, 1985), in which high school students interviewed community members to ground learning and record local history simultaneously.

Joint curriculum design enlists students to express themselves and activate personal data bases. Inductive teaching draws heavily from students to ascertain what is known and help students identify what needs to be known. Individualized input encourages further thought.

In what ways do students express prior knowledge? How do learning experiences build on student knowledge bases?

Throughout my teaching career, I have watched students gain confidence in stating opinions. I have elicited past experiences and urged reconsideration of present conclusions. I have pressed students to think for themselves, to examine opposing viewpoints, and to seek additional information to be able to substantiate ideas at any given point.

A believer in writing to learn, I assign countless writing exercises. Students scribble initial reactions, write and rewrite reasoned reflections on readings, or synthesize conclusions following a heated discussion, keeping a running dialogue with themselves. An inductive approach not only dignifies a learner's thoughts, but allows for a change of mind, based on accumulated evidence over time. With joint curriculum design, students develop critical thinking, listening, and speaking skills in efforts to express ideas and respect differing viewpoints.

Peers—Exchanges

Joint curriculum design values each learner's contributions to the learning process to widen perspectives and deepen understandings.

Sizer's (1985) efforts to restructure secondary schools stemmed from a similar philosophy. His nine principles promoted learner-centered, inductive, affective, integrated learning. Focusing on student, teacher, and content, as a triangle of attention, Sizer proposed "to develop powers of thought, of taste, and of judgment" (p. 4). He wanted to stir student and teacher intellects, imaginations, and consciences to nurture resourceful thinking about important matters.

The continuous growth of Sizer's work evidences faith in learner responsibility. Joint curriculum design follows a similar belief, encouraging students to exert personal responsibility and to discover complementary strengths in others to accomplish shared visions.

In *The Dialectic of Freedom*, Greene (1988) stressed the significance of *humane choosing*, which empowers individuals to go beyond personal desire and accommodation to existing socioeconomic structures, to take the initiative to envision how to effect responsible social change. In addition, Perrone (1991) argued, "There is a need for new understandings that the world, however defined, is not static, that change is possible and that it demands a personal and collective investment" (p. 15). Joint curriculum design challenges students and teachers to develop this two-pronged awareness, to forge ahead with individual drive for cooperative endeavors, to act as agents of change who engineer ways to help others and better society.

How do learners relate? Do assignments provoke individual inquiry and cooperative research? Do learners recognize themselves as resources?

Positive returns result when resources emerge from interaction and teachers free curriculum to accommodate unique perspectives. "Interest, novelty, change, and adventure are exchanged for control, certainty, conformity, stability, order" (Carini, 1991, p. 25). In our study, Lorraine and Sarah found new energy in the depth of student interests and knowledge once they opened curriculum to students who offered new vantage points.

Joint curriculum design presents students with frequent opportunities to display knowledge and talents, individually and together, through cooperative tasks that determine what to study and how to achieve and assess joint goals.

Teachers—Costume Changes

Joint curriculum design asks teachers to model and practice lifelong learning. As the main experts in the room, teachers apply knowledge and training to learning experiences, but they also include students in decision making and learn from them in the process.

Joint curriculum design has roots that stretch back through the 20th century. The idea of teachers and students organizing and negotiating aspects of teaching and learning is not new. As far back as 1942 (Giles, McCuthan, & Zechiel), cooperative planning proved to have powerful consequences:

> Testimony of these teachers [showed] that their growth has been immeasurably stimulated by the questions and problems which students raise; by the aid of students in determining methods of work; by the constant need to discover new materials ... by the increased excellence of student presentations; and by the effort to find new and more valid records and evaluations. (p. 227)

The rewards of cooperative planning were many, but world events ended the Eight-Year Study that occasioned them. Decades later, concepts reappeared and research that delineated cooperative learning (Johnson et al., 1984; Kagan, 1988; Noddings, 1990; Slavin et al., 1985) encouraged students and teachers to utilize positive interdependence, individual and group goals, shared decision making, constructive feedback, and self or joint assessment. Students took a more active part in learning, whereas teachers worked as facilitators.

Joint curriculum design emanates from these past experiences, but raises expectations for students and teachers beyond those of cooperative planning and cooperative learning. Joint curriculum design fosters a more equal partnership through collaborative action research. Role reversals occur, as students and teachers alternately serve as leaders and learners, strengthening the concept of a community of learners (Meier, 1995a).

Lorraine and Sarah discovered students were willing to work much more when they gained a greater say in what they were doing. Students unanimously preferred the change of roles. Students noted the following:

> She's giving us the opportunity to communicate with our fellow peers.

> The teacher has had more time to actually help us with the work and explain more thoroughly the material in question.

> We are not only teaching ourselves but helping other students teach themselves.

> We do more group work, but we actually understand what we're doing better.

Joint curriculum design operates in a democratic classroom, relying on active citizenry and genuine concern for one another.

Joint curriculum design engenders an atmosphere of intellectual stimulation that excites the natural curiosity of students and teachers.

Schools—Lighting

Life is interdisciplinary, yet most secondary learning remains departmentalized. In addition, human resources tend to be narrowly defined and inefficiently tapped. Joint curriculum design relates learning to life and features staff as available, multifaceted resources. Interdisciplinary approaches engender interconnections. Natural links between English and social studies or math and sciences offer integrated learning, but so do thematic approaches across all disciplines. I have seen entire units developed around the study of a period of history, a natural formation, an ecological life cycle. Careful articulation among departments can create investigations filled with lasting learning experiences for students and teachers.

Critical thinking escalates in interdisciplinary inquiry, as do self-regulation and problem solving. Students learn to develop focus, simplify questions, think fluently and flexibly, design experiments, seek patterns, take risks, use metaphors, and cooperate and collaborate (Martinello & Cook, 1994).

Teaming up with colleagues allows teachers similar rewards. *Inquiring communities* bond faculties through professionalism (Sergiovanni, 1994), create nurturing contexts (Noddings, 1984), and improve the quality of learning to attract future educators who perpetuate reflective practice (Sarason, 1993).

Joint curriculum design rejuvenates teachers. Collaborative efforts across disciplines foster a collegial school culture and the joys of learning.

Joint curriculum design sends out positive vibrations through the school and into the community.

Community—Reciprocity

Advantages of collaboration flow in all directions. When students and teachers share in the learning process, they not only inform one another, but also realize the importance of tapping additional resources.

Seeking outside sources poses mutual benefits. Joint sharing of personnel and problems transforms otherwise remote parties into active collaborators. Students learn to corroborate information through primary sources; they learn the channels and protocols for getting things done. Schools and communities develop partnerships that strengthen images, perceptions, and resources.

Kilpatrick's (1925) *project method* integrated classroom experiments of the learner's experience with community campaigns to raise social consciousness. In the 1950s, schools like the Philadelphia Parkway School used city resources to enact high school curriculum (Cox, 1972). Later, Bernstein (1975), Freire (1973, 1991), and Giroux (1988, 1992) described the potential for school to be a socially transformative vehicle in which students learn to question, to risk, to ascertain. Meier (1995b) asserted successful high school reform through *The Power of Their Ideas*, as students, parents, and teachers gained voice in the learning process.

School reform in the 1990s has splintered into magnet schools, charter schools, site-managed schools, information-age schools, mandate-responsive schools, value-driven schools, and schools-within-schools. "The most common features in the framework are staff/parent and community involvement ... " (Walberg & Lane, 1989, p. ix).

Joint curriculum design invites students and teachers to bring in guest speakers, in person or over airwaves, to go out into the community, local or more far-flung. Students and teachers probe deeper into actual situations with added help and expertise. Emotionally charged, real-life, controversial issues spark heated discussions that provide students and teachers opportunities to deal constructively with social and political differences (Barell, 1991; Bateman, 1990). Joint curriculum design propels learning into the real-world arena.

SUMMARY

Human resources add faces, personalities, biases, and beliefs to the learning process. Collaborations allow individual learners to express themselves, while learning from peers, teachers, families, and community members—whether in walking distance or a few computer clicks away.

Behind-the-Scenes Mental Preparation: Suggestions for Learning Log Entries

1. List the last few analogies or metaphors you have employed in teaching. Look for patterns to identify the source of the connections you make. State how students responded to the comparisons made through these interests and examples.

If students lacked recognition, what steps can you take to broaden their understanding?

2. Draw a floor plan of the classroom and graph fixed features. Measure proportional slips of paper for each flexible feature or movable item. Experiment with ways to change the room for more effective learning space.

3. Inventory material resources and review upcoming course topics. Write out ways to incorporate real-world items to illustrate key

concepts. Review the list with a peer to find what other objects might be appropriate.

4. Maintain a card file of the people who have enriched past classes. Document name, date, purpose, and result. Flip through the file to reacquaint yourself with people who successfully broadened student understanding. Search for ways to widen the network. Record priorities by subject for cross reference.

On-Stage Tryouts:
Collaborations With Students

1. Develop a database of student interests and unique experiences. Keep files in computers or on poster paper on bulletin boards to give access to the class as they pursue knowledge. Apply this information and encourage students to do the same when creating analogies or metaphors.

2. Show the floor plan to students and ask for input. Discuss how to use fixed space for mutual benefit and brainstorm ways to move other items for more comfortable and effective surroundings.

Introduce the idea of appointing a class "architect" for a certain span of time charged with how to improve learning areas.

3. Challenge students to relate concepts taught in class to specific items found at home. Have students bring items in and explain the associations they make. Such an exercise not only reveals the student level of comprehension, but also broadens understandings as the whole class sees a concept through another's eyes. Discuss the value of recycling items to evoke other associations for new comparisons or contrasts.

4. Ask each student to identify at least one person who would add to learning related to course content. Have students contact the person, obtain addresses (e-mail, internet, fax, etc.) and phone numbers. Create a class reference file of guest speakers.

8

Rehearsals: Experimentation

ಶಿ ◆ ಜ

Experimentation requires perspective and persistence—learning from seeming mistakes, backtracking to adjust, and starting out again.

Polished performances seem to materialize with ease and naturalness, belying the hard work and repeated rehearsals that precede final productions. Amateur actors may become easily discouraged if they are not aware of the effort professional performers exert to achieve the level of competence audiences witness.

Worthwhile innovations in education fade quickly for similar reasons. Without knowing rationales for specific changes or without training and support to follow through efforts to try something new, veteran and student teachers become discouraged when first attempts fail. Wonderful ideas wither for lack of trying a second time. Hesitancy to experiment restricts learning and affects students who, in turn, fear making mistakes.

Teachers who experiment model inquiry for students. They inspire constructive change. As Ayers (1991) asserted, "It is by means of education that we hope to widen horizons, open perspectives, discover possibilities, and overcome obstacles" (p. 125).

He argued further that "sustained inquiry, formal and informal, is an important part of learning how to teach" (p. 128). **Joint curriculum design** stresses that sustained inquiry and reflection are just as important in learning how to learn. The following description applies to students as well:

> Reflection is a process that can allow teachers to integrate personal, implicit knowledge with objective knowledge ... it is thinking rigorously, critically,

and systematically about practices ... assessing situations, imagining a different future, and preparing to act on that thought." (Ayers, 1991, p. 129).

Joint curriculum design thrives on joint reflective experimentation with curriculum. Students join teachers in rigorous inquiry and reflection regarding subject matter and learning processes. Perspective and persistence prove rewarding.

Like theater rehearsals, with promise of success and possibility for refinements, changes in curricular responsibility and patterns of communication impact knowledge acquisition.

CASTING: COMPLEMENTARY EFFORTS

Joint curriculum design is never static. Students and teachers, as learners, respond to group dynamics and new ideas throughout learning processes. According to talents, abilities, and interests, they select roles to start a unit of study, cognizant that they will alter plans and switch parts as inquiry ensues (see Fig. 3.3). They maintain perspective by reciprocal reinforcement and reaffirmation of the ultimate goal of increased learning. Collaborative **action research** prepares students and teachers for casting and recasting.

Despite careful planning, actors and researchers know that unforeseen events or circumstances alter original intentions—often for better results. Students and teachers, too, prepare for unplanned changes in direction and emphases. They design learning experiences in a spirit of flexibility and trust (see chapter 4). Joint curriculum design flourishes in a climate of voiced differences and the unexpected.

As Fig. 8.1 illustrates, joint curriculum design causes chain reactions among learners similar to those that occur in a theater community as players tryout for parts and interpret readings. **Choices** regarding content and resources lead to **adjustments** based on **practice** and **feedback**.

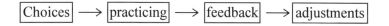

FIG. 8.1. The chain reaction of experimentation in joint curriculum design.

Joint curriculum design inspires **critical pedagogy**. Discovery learning and problem-solving, not perfection, propel experimentation. A system of checks and network of people guide implementation, provide feedback, and effect change in a supportive and thoughtful climate.

Choices—Content and Resources

Experimenting with joint curriculum design causes students and teachers to examine choices and decisions, as well as consequences of interchanging roles.

The throes of change can be disconcerting unless regular, open dialogue occurs to express concerns and insights from multiple viewpoints. Without exchange, frustration mounts. With candidness, minor glitches are resolved before tensions rise. Regular debriefings maintain the flow for joint curriculum design.

After a full month of experimenting with joint curriculum design, Lorraine and Sarah polled students about their impressions regarding choices and change.

Cooperative Learning—Forming Groups. Students raised concerns about fair work distribution in cooperative learning experiences. They liked groupwork, but sought autonomy in choosing group members.

Lorraine expressed ambivalence, explaining to them:

> I agree with some of your ideas, but not all … most of you were involved and were following through … some were not involved … I saw a number of occasions when people who usually don't work in this class were working and that was good … I'm not sure yet whether more work is done in assigned or unassigned groups … I did see many of you helping each other.

Joint evaluation of reactions and differences of opinion reassured students that their input mattered. Mutual respect caused students to consider Lorraine's observations and their responsibility for insuring success. Discussing implementation issues with students raised the level of cooperative learning by demonstrating the effectiveness of dialogue.

Similar concerns arose when Sarah discussed initial changes with students. Given choice, students preferred groupwork, but weighed advantages with disadvantages. They enjoyed "talking about the subject, trying to understand it better, working with all types of people." However, they complained about "who you're working with. They may be uncooperative or inattentive or lazy."

After this discussion of drawbacks, students resolved to remedy the situation by monitoring one another to guarantee that everyone contributed to group efforts. They enlisted Sarah's assistance with more difficult classmates, who often worked better in self-selected groups. The chance to raise issues and reach resolution facilitated a renewed environment for learning.

When we addressed this issue, Lorraine, Sarah, and I focused on greater learner choice and responsibility to increase learning. We stressed positive interdependence, as described by Johnson and Johnson (1991), to create effective environments in which groups performed well whether randomly selected or student-generated.

Joint curriculum design afforded students and teachers opportunities to discuss cooperation and social skills in conjunction with affective and cognitive learning.

What situations or circumstances have caused discussions and compromises as you experiment?

Integration of Skills and Content. Presentation of information can facilitate comprehension and spur on further pursuit of knowledge. "The inquiry approach is characterized overall by an intensive investigation of central issues or problems, and strives for a balanced interweaving of process and content" (Cook, 1991, p. 149). Joint curriculum design stresses integral learning.

Examples of this concept arose when Lorraine introduced the four-paragraph essay and peer editing at the same time. Previously, she had not believed students had the ability to edit and revise each other's writing, so she had never allowed students to exchange working drafts. In this instance, she surprised herself by relinquishing control. Students worked industriously, challenging one another to clarify points and delve deeper into ideas. Results gratified everyone.

Final drafts evidenced a higher level of student thought and expression than in the past. Hindsight helped Lorraine realize that her previous emphasis on form when introducing the longer essay had precluded student concern with content. Whereas, peer review over form and content sparked better crafted writing of substance. Grades increased 10 to 15 points higher than former writing assignments these students had completed.

Joint curriculum design had prompted personalized learning and increased autonomy, expression, critical thinking, and success.

What strategies have enabled learners to incorporate content while improving necessary academic skills?

Concerns—Measuring Learning.   A different situation arose between Sarah and her students. They fought the three-unit, 100-short-answer vocabulary test they faced every marking period. They protested that 60 words were too many, class test time was too short, and exam questions too difficult. They reasoned strenuously, but Sarah could not imagine making up exams and then spending more time to grade them, when prepared, scoring-machine tests seemed so convenient.

Sarah struggled with this request because she saw the student frustration level and repeated failure. She compromised by giving only 50 questions from printed exams, and students grades did improve. Students remained disgruntled though, anxious to change format even more. They resisted studying words for a test, rather than for understanding for future use (see chapter 9).

Joint curriculum design opened up dialogue regarding curricular decisions and allowed for negotiation and compromise that had not existed in the past.

What content issues have you negotiated with students in your first attempts at implementing joint curriculum design?

Adjustments—Inquiry and Research

Attempts to negotiate curriculum open areas for discourse unfamiliar to students and teachers. Twists and turns keep the mobile of joint curriculum design elements in motion (see chapter 2). **Inquiry** and **research** affect interrelationships among **goals** and **methods**. As collaboration increases, adjustments occur.

Inquiry—Curricular Decisions and Outcomes.   When learners inquire into curricular decisions and outcomes, as teachers and students do in joint curriculum design, they interrogate all aspects of learning. Critical pedagogy encourages questioning of content, instruction, and activities. As McLaren (1995) described, teachers strive to help students critically engage the politics and ideologies which inform these questions, as they begin to understand themselves as both a product and producer of meaning ..." (p. 15).

Joint curriculum design builds the foundation from which students recognize the power of their input. Rather than remain docile, students learn they have the right and responsibility to speak up.

As Lorraine and Sarah continued to experiment with joint curriculum design, open discussions enabled them to monitor their own roles, as well as counsel students about how to help themselves. Students who had been restive in the sedentary ways they had long endured became proactive. Joint curriculum design enabled them to readjust concepts of learning. The quest for knowledge led them to probe deeper and develop activities without prompting. They strove to achieve the goals for more independence that they had indicated on initial surveys (see chapter 5).

Lorraine remarked: "The kids are fair—if given a voice, they recognize what they've done and what they haven't done." She wavered at times, but caught herself when she did revert to former ways: "I'm spending a lot of time talking again ... when the posters went up, instead of letting them tell me, I was telling them."

Lorraine's increasing trust in herself, students, and joint curriculum design surfaced and resurfaced. Even in the face of regression, which happens, she learned to assess the consequences of her actions. The previous remark described Period 3, but by Period 5 that same day, she altered her approach and elicited more student response.

Lorraine succeeded in readjusting her concept of teaching. She labored to break the traditional mold that had restricted her. She revived early teaching memories of student-centered learning and improved on them with collaborative curricular choices through joint curriculum design. She shared her expertise while eliciting and dignifying student knowledge and interests.

Overall, Lorraine and her students eagerly created a community of learners. Conscious awareness of underlying themes—investigation and personalization (see chapter 5) altered the classroom climate. Increased responsibility facilitated and increased ownership.

In contrast to former isolating and competitive modes of instruction, joint curriculum design caused the classroom to buzz with purposeful activities, conducted in conjunction with others, which renewed relevance and student incentive.

Have you found that students have developed greater motivation for learning? Have they applied greater social awareness to studies? Have they displayed greater independence?

Research—Curiosity. Research entails uncovering knowns and discovering unknowns. Researchers examine ideas, develop hypotheses, test possibilities, apply insights, draw conclusions. Action research into all aspects of teaching revives teacher curiosity and heightens student awareness. Questions arise regarding what topics or subtopics may have been emphasized, skirted or overlooked. Because teachers and students co-research curriculum, joint curriculum design activates a spirit of inquiry that develops into ongoing research.

Sarah's classes responded immediately and well to gaining a say in their own learning. Previously, they had been expending energy to behave, largely out of respect for Sarah, but had not been actively involved in class purposes. With joint curriculum design, students felt freer to connect with each other and the material, to offer opinions, and to seek feedback. Their positive reactions, along with steady support from Lorraine and myself, reassured Sarah to sustain the change effort.

A newfound sense of joint exploration grew steadily through actual experience with joint curriculum design. Readings, discussions, and reflections helped Sarah to appreciate her strengths, student input, and the powerful differences that change had wrought. Student drive, initiative, and creativity delighted her; student ability to interact positively surprised her. Fears about learner accountability lessened considerably. Relieved to be able to loosen a tight grip, Sarah displayed her lively personality and keen intelligence.

Students approached school work enthusiastically. They learned how to formulate research questions, use media resources, consult with classmates, and arrive at new understandings. Freedom to experiment with learning experiences caught imaginations and nourished curiosity.

Joint curriculum design created a domino effect. Sarah raised expectations for all students and students proved worthy of greater trust. As a team, Sarah and her students began to share the enjoyment of learning for which they all aspired.

How have class attitudes and interests changed? Have learners pursued content to a greater degree? Have they consulted with one another regarding new information?

Practice—Collaboration

As joint curriculum design unfolds, students pose problems and probe issues. They learn through practical experience that inquiry and research are unpredictable. They learn to refine research questions and to redirect efforts. Teachers learn to become facilitators, not dispensers, of knowledge.

Students as Collaborators. Collaboration requires more from individuals than cooperative learning does. Collaboration assumes equal status, mutual responsibility, intellectual endeavors. Joint curriculum design quickly moves beyond cooperative learning as curricular decision making prods teachers and students to achieve genuine collaboration.

For example, Sarah's students wrote journal entries about their reading habits prior to the study. They candidly admitted to not reading at all, renting movies, or reading only parts of stories. Some claimed to have reached eighth grade without ever reading an entire assigned book. Collaborating changed some attitudes:

> I read more this time than the other books … What made me read more was the maps because I didn't want not to read anything and when I had to do the maps have no idea what to do.

> I feel I would pass a test on *Johnny Tremain* because the groups we were in helped explain things I didn't read yet. Then when I read it, I understood it more.

> I read up to Chapter 10 and I will finish it before Friday. I know it better because of the mappings and posters. We also wrote what we thought of some of the chapters and traded with others. I liked doing this book better because of all the groupwork.

Joint curriculum design had raised the stakes. No one could easily hide from an entire class. These teenagers did not want to be embarrassed among their peers, so some actually accomplished more for their groups than they had previously done for themselves.

Have more students become actively involved in preparing for and contributing to classwork? What circumstances caused these changes? How do these changes manifest themselves?

Teachers as Facilitators. When Lorraine's students analyzed two different texts simultaneously, she felt "uncomfortable about not reviewing all the facts about both books." Even though she realized students were applying higher critical thinking levels by voluntarily comparing and contrasting both works, she wondered if they were being shortchanged. In one of our discussions, talking out loud seemed to help Lorraine resolve her own conflict:

> Moving and working cooperatively, I think they are starting to get used to it. I see signs where they know what we're doing and they realize … but I think some of them think they are getting away with things … they are more relaxed … it's not that they're doing any less than when I did the regular work … the only difference now is more are working.

Lorraine's remarks were self-revelatory. Initial concerns gave way to slipping into former patterns of thinking, as she unconsciously reverted to language that reflected she had previously done all the work! In a journal entry, Lorraine described how her role changed:

> I *have become* an organizer of materials, a director of initiating projects, a source of information, a surveyor of progress. The process of initiating groups involves:
>
> 1) setting up rules, guidelines for activities;
> 2) teaching necessary information so groups can work;
> 3) supervising groups to help students channel their efforts to fruitful conclusions;
> 4) evaluating groupwork.
>
> My role has changed from doing all the work to setting up the experience so students can do the work.

Lorraine had inductively internalized adjustments. With practice, she had reestablished her position on the educational stage in terms of joint curriculum design. She realized joint control had altered her role and had increased student responsibility in the learning process.
What insights have arisen in your experiences with reflective research regarding curriculum decision making?

Interdisciplinary Investigations. Interdisciplinary investigations evolve within the inquiry and research aspects of joint curriculum design. Martinello and Cook (1994) offered thematic studies based on student-generated topics as alternatives in which students gain voice within teacher-framed options. Joint curriculum design elevates this alternative to a regular instructional strategy, shared with teachers.

When Sarah first broached a unit surrounding *Johnny Tremain*, students eagerly shared information gained from recent social studies lessons about the Revolutionary War. Student enthusiasm prompted Sarah to brainstorm ideas for interdisciplinary projects. Students proudly pursued investigations of the Revolutionary War to interpret events in the storyline. This integration of prior knowledge coupled with new inquiries into the place and times of the novel strengthened student learning. Presentations of findings enriched class discussions.

Joint curriculum design crossed traditional lines and raised relevance beyond single disciplines. Practice in inquiry and research broadened learner discoveries, associative thinking, and research capabilities.

How has course content been integrated with other studies? What interdisciplinary projects have developed? Have more colleagues attempted joint curriculum design?

Feedback—Communication

Frequent polling of students maintains momentum for joint curriculum design. Without regular conversations, teachers easily revert to full decision making. Sudden shutdowns could cause students to sense a loss of trust. Open, active communication averts such misunderstanding.

At the end of the first quarter in which they introduced joint curriculum design, Lorraine and Sarah polled students for feedback regarding specific changes, learning aids, and possible problems. Earlier inquiries had provided unexpected replies (see chapters 5 and 6). Students volunteered comments on a daily basis, but both teachers sought to confirm their own observations about comfort levels for all students regarding ongoing change.

Specific Changes. Though Lorraine and Sarah experienced different reactions to and from each class, they decided to ask all

students similar open-ended questions. Thoughtful full-length para-
graphs contrasted with previous surveys that produced fragmentary
remarks at first and mere single sentence replies a month later. Work
samples had evidenced similar improved facility with language.
Varied activities and experiences inspired by joint curriculum design
had encouraged **critical literacy**.

Lorraine's students identified the following changes: more confidence in writing and speaking, better study habits, more enjoyable
classtime, greater variety in assignments, more diverse expressions
of learning, and greater familiarity with classmates.

Sarah's students identified changes in the use of time, student
choice of topic and seating, working together and helping each other,
more activity, greater involvement in class discussions, more cooperation among themselves, greater variety of visual aids, better
grades, and less need for disciplining!

Joint curriculum design had awakened student interest in educational goals and methods of learning entrusted to their care. Students
became more aware of surroundings and their contributions to the
learning environment (see chapter 4). They became more attuned
to precision in expressing ideas. Once their impressions could be
voiced and considered, students exhibited greater alertness, sensitivity, and reliability.

**How frequently do you poll students to ascertain their im-
pressions of the effects of experimentation and change? How
do student reactions compare over time?**

Critics have challenged the rosy pictures that joint curriculum
design consistently suggests, yet my experience constantly reaffirms
benefits for teachers and students.

Learning Aids.   Besides listing noticeable changes, explicit
mention of aids to learning assists students and teachers in maintaining awareness of metacognition. Joint curriculum design succeeds as long as teachers and students are learners who continue
to recognize how they learn best. All classes clearly identified
strategies that had improved their access to knowledge.

Lorraine's classes felt more comfortable working closely with
classmates, getting and giving help; they found classwork more
interesting and liked organizing ideas in writing. Greater intercom-
munication created a friendlier atmosphere. They believed grades
had improved because greater effort resulted in learning more.

Sarah's classes recognized the following advantages: less time wasted, better comprehension of material, more help from more people more often, greater cooperation, more participation, better visualization of information, and more work completed with apparently less effort. They especially enjoyed seeing things from other perspectives, delving deeper into chosen topics, presenting ideas and reports, and wanting to pay more attention.

Joint curriculum design had empowered learners. They not only increased their interest in learning, but also reaped benefits of working in a community of learners. These positive replies proved more optimistic than either Lorraine or Sarah had thought possible.

What new learning aids have facilitated knowledge acquisition? How closely do your perceptions match those of students?

Problems Created by Change. How could so many different individuals in distinctly different grade levels and courses arrive at similar conclusions? Generally speaking, an approach to learning that allows for differentiation and individualization, as joint curriculum design does, pleases more people than not. Choice and collaboration are strong motivators. Adjustable time frames and selected topics afford ownership and greater opportunities for success.

Lorraine's classes proved unanimous in their opinion regarding change. Despite difficulties with cooperative learning roles in the beginning, they asserted that they had not experienced any other problems. They preferred group learning and appreciated gaining a voice in curriculum.

The majority of Sarah's students emphatically felt they had not experienced problems either. However, a handful of students did mention occasional difficulties in getting one's point across or trying to get a group to agree, or working in assigned groups, which meant working with people they didn't know or didn't care to know. These concerns revealed increased awareness of critical literacy—reciprocal speaking and listening.

A few of Sarah's students doubted themselves and classmates, unsure if they were learning "the right things, the right way." They feared the possibility that "the whole group could get things wrong." These wary students approached change cautiously. They admitted that their grades had gone up, but wondered if the trend would continue. Grades did indicate improved degrees of learning. Voiced concerns prompted response.

Sarah allayed student worries on an individual basis, helping students to recognize the sense of community that had evolved because they did work together to pursue joint endeavors. Increased awareness of classmates and differences in learners encouraged students to reach out to help one another succeed. Additional reassurance stemmed from the fact that Sarah was always available to verify group learning.

Joint curriculum design improved student learning to a greater extent than Lorraine or Sarah had hoped. They appreciated positive gains, but sought strategies to help doubters feel more confident and comfortable.

WORKING ENSEMBLES: MULTIPLE VERSIONS

Casting characters assumes willing participants, but not all learners seek the limelight. Some prefer to work behind the scenes, in the background, or independently. Luring learners into action does not necessitate putting everyone on center stage. Other options exist.

Joint curriculum design honors various approaches to content to make sense of curriculum. Individual interpretations and self-expression form one level of understanding; combined understandings and multiple expressions contribute another level of knowing. Choice invites learners to develop critical literacy through individual and joint learning experiences.

Figure 8.2 represents the overlapping nature of critical pedagogy—**inquiry** and **research**, **collaboration** and **communication**, with elements of critical literacy.

Critical literacy underscores reading, writing, speaking, and listening. Joint curriculum design urges learners to practice critical literacy through **self-expression** and respect for multiple **perspectives**.

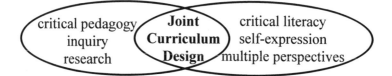

FIG. 8.2. Overlapping elements of critical pedagogy and critical literacy.

Self-Expression—Considerations

Impetuousness and impatience characterize youth, but need not remain the norm. Through research, adolescents learn to temper responses, to nurture patience and persistence. Joint curriculum design gives teenagers countless opportunities to assert themselves and analyze consequences of thoughts and actions.

As casting and recasting of roles assist ensembles in producing a performance, interchanging roles in joint curriculum design facilitates learning. Role switching enables teachers and students to gain perspective.

In journal entries, Lorraine's students identified distinctions and benefits of role reversals caused by joint curriculum design:

> Since February, I think the teacher's work has decreased. She does less writing on the board. Also she doesn't have to explain things as many times. So she's doing less talking. Our job has changed for the better. We do more group work, but we actually understand what we're doing better ...

> She doesn't teach us as much any more. We mostly teach ourselves now. This puts much more pressure on us and takes some pressure off the teacher ... now with the groupwork, we are not only teaching ourselves but helping other students teach themselves.

> Before February, the teacher just stood in the front of the class, but now she walks around the room to see how these changes are affecting us to catch mistakes early. Since her job changed, we can't socialize as much and pay attention more.

> Since February, the teacher has had more time to actually help us with the work and explain more thoroughly the material in question.

Students realized that they thought and worked more seriously. They appreciated collaborative decision making, learning social skills along with academics.

Before Lorraine read these student journal entries, she recorded her own reflections:

> English class became less tedious, less of a pull between myself and the class. ... I felt a shift from curriculum orientation to student orientation. I didn't need to teach everything on the list—the curriculum had to be adjusted to the students' learning patterns. ... I was amazed at how some children had a chance to shine who had seemed failures in the past. Poster work and group

projects tapped other creative sources ... the students seem to feel better about themselves ...

What students *think* I'm doing differently:

1. not talking so much;
2. giving students more power in the choices of what we will do;
3. evaluating students differently;
4. formulating differently how we will learn.

Students' jobs have changed—THEY DO MORE—THEY LEARN MORE.

Lorraine reached her original goal of including students in the "magic circle of learning." Joint curriculum design had redirected her efforts and raised her expectations for all students. Perhaps most telling was including herself as learner—signalling a genuine community of learners alive and well.

Perspectives—Contributions

Joint curriculum design demands attention to patterns of communication to facilitate clarity and cogency. Students who design learning appreciate self-expression and welcome comments and contributions from others. Extending critical literacy, learners must speak clearly and listen attentively to construe and construct meaning.

Sarah found noticeable differences in student work. She shared insights with an assistant principal who had observed her class involved in interdisciplinary studies: "Everybody got involved and interacted with the material and was making judgments ... I never thought the kids would come up with this ... to compare themes to modern day ... I never got so much before ..." Sarah's students concurred:

We learn as a group and she [Sarah] just makes sure we understand.

We are working together to get something done, depending on each other to get the answers, like in real life.

We're uniting, we're becoming like family. For those who are quiet, like me, it's hard to communicate with others and the groupwork is helping people find talents that they know they didn't have.

Students reaped rewards of pooling ideas and analyzing possibilities. They felt more secure with active participation and ideas agreed on by classmates; critical thinking challenged them to perform consistently at higher levels. As Martinello and Cook (1994) asserted: "Brainstorming involves thinking fluently and flexibly, habits of mind that are important to productive inquiry. ... New perspectives help thinking become more fluent and flexible" (p. 83).

Joint curriculum design strengthened thinking, sharing, and synthesizing. Students and teachers recognized that differing viewpoints sparked livelier class discussions and more thought-provoking writings.

SUMMARY

This chapter presented details of ongoing implementation of joint curriculum design, as perceived by students and teachers. Action research into increased curricular decision making sparked critical pedagogy as well as critical literacy.

Behind-the-Scenes Mental Preparation

1. Review initial student suggestions for change and chart how students' ideas have been addressed and received. Develop questions you think students might ask regarding what has changed and whether or not more changes would be welcome.

2. Review your early entries in your learning log to identify early concerns and questions. List those that have been satisfactorily met and those that still require additional thought. Sketch strategies to address these latter concerns or questions with students.

3. Consider the theater metaphor of casting and recasting roles to create working ensembles that produce more effective performances. How has implementing joint curriculum design sustained this metaphor?

On-Stage Tryouts:

1. Refer students to the chart of concerns that they prioritized at the start of joint curriculum design (based on Activity 3, chapter 2).

Discuss changes that have improved learning and list concerns that still arise. Discuss how to continue to improve.

2. Share your concerns with students, if they differ from theirs, and discuss how to alleviate these concerns through specific, practical changes—by consensus.

3. Ask students to read early journal entries for two purposes: (a) to note issues and (b) to note language use. Then, ask students to peruse more recent entries for the same two purposes. Have students write a comparison to indicate what they have learned about learning and about language. Pair students to share insights; then, hold a whole-class discussion of differences noted.

9

Performances:
Ongoing Authentic Assessment

ಬಿ ◆ ೞ

Previews precede theatrical performances, as ongoing authentic assessments by teachers, students, and peers inform and mark progress toward learning.

After weeks of rehearsals, performers run through previews to gain self-knowledge and improve efforts before exposing their work to opening-night audiences, reviews, and ratings. Ongoing, authentic assessment informs the quality of final presentations—a practice adopted and promoted by educational reformers.

Formerly, norm-based, evaluative testing restricted concepts of learning, leaving many students outside the mainstream. Good memorizers and test-takers outshone global or original thinkers; sequential learners appeared more adept than random or abstract learners. IQ tests or S.A.T. exams favored some intelligences and cultures over others, ignoring individual, criteria-based, and formative learning. Quantitative tests and measurements recorded specific information, but overlooked qualitative growth and achievement.

Learning is no longer gauged by a few isolated and arbitrary test scores. Timed examinations and short-answer tests lack sufficient scope to indicate levels of knowledge. Numerical results fail to provide feedback regarding what to improve. Instead, students, peers, and teachers monitor and appraise progress through ongoing, authentic measures before learning outcomes are presented to local evaluators, outside audiences, or experts.

Assessment has broadened from reliance on standardized tests and measurements of discrete, discipline-linked facts to inclusion of demonstrations and exhibitions of knowledge that evidence individual competence, creativity, interdisciplinary connections, and intellectual growth. Pop quizzes and midterm or final examinations are being replaced by cumulative work folders, self-reports, peer evaluations, teacher–student conferences, and projects or portfolios.

Authentic assessments encompass real-life contexts, multistage problems, critical thinking, problem-solving skills, and justifications for response (Wiggins, 1993)—advantages worth noting. Rather than stress weaknesses, assessments are holistic and constructive.

Joint curriculum design supports broader assessment measures, as a logical extension of curricular choices and changes. Self-expression and creativity, individual input and satisfaction, collaboration and heightened social awareness, and flexibility and fluency in dealing with ideas require multiple formats to showcase learning.

Joint curriculum design values negotiated **processes**, alerting students and teachers to **signs of learning** as points of understanding. Learners study **substance**, uncover **suppositions**, and practice **debriefings**. They produce **projects** and **portfolios** to display learning, and submit work to **reviews** for feedback. Ongoing, authentic assessment and collaborative learning stimulate **construction of knowledge**, **reflectiveness**, and **social awareness**, shaping individual and common understandings.

PREVIEWS

Human minds explore ideas on various levels. Randomness and order characterize thought processes. While concentrating on one set of ideas, learners may surprisingly reach conclusions or gain insights about seemingly unrelated topics or concepts. In contrast, ordered, sequential procedures provoke deductive or inductive learning.

Joint curriculum design acknowledges stream of consciousness and logical organization as alternate routes to learning. In addition to intuition and reason, cultural values and customs, personal preferences and predilections guide learner interactions. Authentic assessments document and track development of thought on an individual basis, revealing learner strengths and talents. See Fig. 9.1.

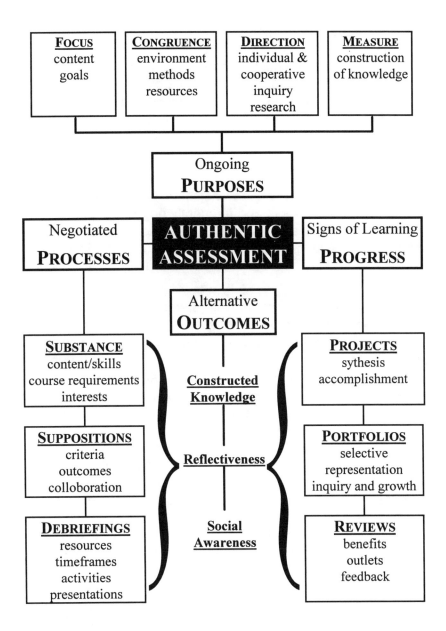

FIG. 9.1. Authentic assessment features of joint curriculum design.

Joint curriculum design is comprehensive. Issues of assessment are not reserved for the end of a unit of study, but figure into course design from the outset. In efforts to establish, measure, and maintain focus, direction, and congruence of curriculum elements (see chapter 2), students and teachers determine clear criteria for expected outcomes before investigation begins. In a dynamic process, they estimate progress and negotiate changes as individual or group needs arise.

Substance—Coursework

Joint curriculum design affords choice of learning experiences, within course requirements and frequently negotiated parameters. As learners, teachers and students pursue interests, acquire information, exercise judgment, and interrogate content to mutually determined ends. They facilitate learning through joint ownership.

Joint Project Design. An earlier reference to the tenth-grade class that faced research writing for the first time reflects joint project design. I introduced the idea of studying ethnic writers who represented student heritage; the class negotiated assignment criteria. They decided to select one writer, read at least one major work and five literary criticisms, write a research paper, and present findings to the class. To attain these goals, they met course requirements for learning research skills.

Content Selections. Students requested class library time to locate authors and commentaries. Self-discovery and research angles produced unique experiences. At first, Irish students selected James Joyce, Italian students chose Dante. I did not dissuade them, but watched as they tested levels of difficulty and discovered other writers. They read Sean O'Casey and Primo Levy, whose works they encouraged their families to read as well. A Jewish student, delighted in finding Isaac Bashevis Singer, read everything she could find by him and discussed his work with grandparents. One adopted Korean student failed to find authors in local libraries. His quest led to a biology teacher offering her husband's personal library. Like a scavenger hunt, the breadth of topics caused students to involve others in their search.

Time Frames.   We sketched out a suitable time frame. Due dates for outlines, abstracts, introductions, and drafts remained flexible because intricacies of research redirected efforts and students progressed at different rates. Students factored in time allotments for planning and rehearsing class presentations, designating specific due dates for project termination.

Introducing Skills.   Research skills comprised a common core of content learning for the unit, but learners determined when to focus on that aspect. They requested instruction on how to gather and organize information on a need-to-know basis. I outlined research methods and procedures that students adapted to their needs, topics, and learning styles. Choice broadened group appreciation for the breadth of research possibilities.

Classtime Activities.   Classtime activities varied as students sought additional information in the library or continued writing in the computer lab, while others read and took notes in the classroom. I served as a resource person—discussing readings, suggesting research options, or reviewing written drafts.

Ethnic connections stimulated pride in students with similar backgrounds. Choice of genre led some to self-select into groups interested in poetry, drama, or fiction. Chronological connections led others to compare contemporaneous lives and styles of writing. Groupwork had not been planned originally, but grew out of student-initiated common bonds.

Students designed formats to present their research to classmates who evaluated each project for substance, originality, organization, and clarity. Skits, readings, and panels celebrated ethnicities, research, world literature, and learner achievement.

Outcomes.   Joint curriculum design invited students to delve into different time periods, literary genres, and ethnic writers, while learning how to research. Individually and in groups, students exercised ongoing assessment of information, progress, pacing, and methods of learning. Operating at the higher end of Bloom's taxonomy, they analyzed, synthesized, and evaluated sources and resources, drafts, peer efforts, and finished projects. Excitement of learning, bred by choice and nurtured by sustained support, charged students for weeks of individualized and cooperative learning.

How have choice and joint decision making sparked learner interest in research? What areas of expertise have students developed and shared?

Suppositions—Signs of Learning

By applying authentic assessment measures, joint curriculum design alerts learners to the idiosyncratic nature of learning. Rather than rely on universal answers, students and teachers reconceptualize learning and consider conclusions as tentative and susceptible to change. Rather than concentrate on test scores, they appreciate the complexity of the intellectual process they undertake in acquiring knowledge.

Concepts of Learning. Sarah reconsidered assessment. Originally, she had supposed that (a) every learner had to learn the same material and (b) only uniform testing finalized learning and registered results. Over the course of applying joint curriculum design, Sarah realized that collaboration and authentic assessment provided more particularized information that facilitated individual learning.

When students evidenced learning in projects that evolved from analyzing *Johnny Tremain*, Sarah surprised herself and students by not giving a final test on the book. Instead, students gained enriched understandings by exchanging viewpoints—a refreshing twist that caused them to exercise and defend reasoned judgments.

Repeated success prompted Sarah to spread joint curriculum design to all five classes. Choice caused students to consider what they wanted to gain from activities and how to achieve those ends. Eleventh graders role played scenes from *Hamlet* and analyzed character motivations; ninth-grade classes produced artistic visuals of myths they had been reading. Again, obvious learning occurred; no tests were administered.

Lorraine experienced similar reactions. Students became so engrossed in the pursuit of knowledge that she hesitated to interrupt them for the sake of accumulating isolated grades from artificial means:

> getting way off the traditional route ... I'm thinking of eliminating vocabulary tests ... get the book they paid for done, but not test every unit ... expose them to the words ... give them choice as to which unit to be tested on.

Ironically, though joint curriculum design alters views of testing, assessment occurs more frequently, consistently and constructively. As teachers circulate, they engage more directly and individually with students, they proffer more pertinent and immediate feedback. At the same time, students ask more searching questions in a more informal and productive climate, rather than fear looking foolish in a formal, competitive setting.

Assessment Purposes. Ongoing assessment clarifies goals, streamlines methods, redirects inquiry. Interim reports, reviews, reflections, and conferencing focus teachers and students as learners. Teachers estimate student progress more holistically, helping students identify individual strengths and areas for improvement. One-on-one advice and relating fortifies learner resolve and success.

What alternatives have you developed with students to monitor and assess learning? How has ongoing assessment altered suppositions about course content coverage and methods of learning?

Debriefings—Interim Reports

Regular debriefings are integral to joint curriculum design. Students and teachers discuss viewpoints, goals, actions, and results of learning experiences. They share information and feedback, orally and in writing.

Record Keeping. Joint curriculum design entails careful record keeping as students and teachers test hypotheses and draw tentative conclusions. As learners, they collect data in work folders for periodic review. They verify beliefs through research, dialectic journal entries, and conferencing; they record reflections in learning logs. Organized records facilitate information processing.

Work folders contain notes, drafts, explanations and reflections, practice and homework exercises, exams, and final products. These compilations indicate areas of weakness and strength, problems and attempted solutions, challenges and still unanswered questions.

Regular review of contents and conferencing about concerns transform these collections into valuable charts of process and progress. Exchange of ideas and focused interactions instigate further inquiry. Documentation and dialoguing facilitate long- and short-range learning.

What forms of record keeping have developed? What signs of learning have surfaced from regular reviews of records that uniform testing could not reveal?

Rapport. Throughout years of implementing joint curriculum design, I have found that frequent debriefings develop and sustain a lively and open rapport between teachers and students, demystifying access to acknowledge.

Students have rarely been asked to evaluate their own work or the progress of others. They need guidance and reassurance about how to critique efforts in a fruitful, nonjudgmental manner that advances learning without undermining the learner. Positive affective and social dimensions of learning strengthen cognitive learning.

By the second half of the semester, Lorraine and Sarah enlisted students in debriefing each other's work. After students developed specific criteria, they provided logical reasons for constructive criticisms regarding their work and that of peers. Lively conversations about course content resulted in stating differing viewpoints. Increased facility in language use continued to be evident, as students verbalized ideas more precisely.

Students have some experience with end-of-semester or end-of-year evaluations of a course, but they benefit more from interim evaluations that allow for immediate adjustment. One student teacher received the following written midsemester advice from a student:

> When you have us do active things to help us understand what you are teaching us, it is fun to do .... Sometimes you talk too much, but if you have people do active things then they won't mind.

Opportunity to offer opinions permits students to respond frankly to a teacher's concern for effectiveness. Like holding up a mirror, debriefings shed light from various angles that might otherwise not be noted.

Risk Taking. Joint curriculum design encourages risk taking. Students and teachers face new challenges when regular evaluation procedures are supplemented by or forfeited for more authentic assessment alternatives. Reciprocal sensitivity and support cultivate measures of learning that stretch far beyond preset notions and uniform practices.

When Lorraine collaborated with students regarding assessment issues, they expressed concerns and posed solutions. They varied goals and time limits for completion of work to respect individual rates of comprehension. They replaced printed textbook questions with open-ended essay questions, to invite original thought and produce fresh insights through testing.

Not all measures met with equal support. Group grading received mixed reactions. Collaborative personalities enjoyed the option, but grade-conscious students protested. To succeed, they had to develop interdependence (see chapter 8). Group ventures require carefully articulated criteria and equal distribution of work. The rewards of pooling ideas and creating many-faceted answers eventually allayed student fears.

For those students and parents who resist group grades, I have encouraged negotiated choices over time. Students select certain activities to work on alone and other activities in which they will collaborate. Negotiation includes interested parents to further reinforce benefits of collaboration. This conciliatory approach switches the focus away from grades toward learning how to work with others—necessary preparation for the professions and work world, which increasingly prize cooperative projects and joint decision making.

What differences have alternatives to testing created in class climate? How have new criteria for learner success been developed and articulated? What differences in student achievement have emerged?

Accountability.   Joint curriculum design integrates learning that fosters a sense of achievement. Ongoing, authentic assessment affords learners steady support from which to gauge factual and intellectual clarity, urging them to proceed with confidence. They trace patterns of information and strands of thoughts, linking ideas to sharpen focus and direct learning.

On the other hand, teachers gain perspective, too. One math student teacher checked her perceptions against student actions in a tenth-grade geometry class:

> I think I placed the period 5/6 class in a deficit model ... [they] didn't really
> listen to what I had to say and never really did any work .... Today, I think

they shattered that view ... many were asking questions and really trying to understand what they were doing. The best part was that most of the questions were coming from students who I would least expect to ask questions, just because I thought they were the least interested. I'm so excited to see my view is being proven wrong!

Debriefings led to a better appreciation and more accurate reading of student ability than intermittent glimpses produced by homework or testing. This student teacher continued to expect active learning even though students had disappointed her. Her consistent approach transmitted positive signals to learners who realized the need for active participation and increased involvement.

Joint curriculum design inspires ongoing attention to assessment, which alters attitudes in the classroom. Debriefings feature individual awareness. Teachers acquire more information from students who realize greater accountability. Judging progress against jointly developed criteria provides perspective for teachers and students, as does critiquing the work of others.

Joint curriculum design promotes regular debriefing so students and teachers confront issues, dispel misconceptions, and engage in more effective pursuit of knowledge. Debriefings reinforce collaboration.

How often do debriefings concern material and methods? What insights have been gleaned? What adjustments have resulted?

PRESENTATIONS

The elements of joint curriculum design coalesce in presentations. Finished products reveal the extent of planning, depth of investigation, and degree of collaboration that brought ideas to fruition. However, rarely are presentations accepted as final. Performance represents progress, always open to further exploration.

Joint curriculum design unites students and teachers in incorporating learning and curricular components into a coherent whole. Students exhibit synthesis of learning through projects and portfolios that they have carefully prepared for presentation. Debates, interviews, panels, role plays, research papers, or visual representations reflect individual and group learning. Review extends knowledge toward future endeavors.

Projects—Synthesis of Learning

Joint curriculum design celebrates syntheses of learning. Projects represent collaborative planning, individual investigation, and group sharing of new knowledge. Learners express results and findings for which they have invested intensive time and energy. They present information to articulate a viewpoint, obtain recognition, and invite constructive feedback.

Originality. Through joint curriculum design, collaborative project planning and execution cultivate originality. Learners create formats that consider resources, content choices, audiences, and outcomes.

In my supervisory experience, one particular project stands out. Tenth graders wrote children's books, which they illustrated and bound. They initiated an author's fair at a local elementary school to read their books to age groups for which writing was intended. They courted audience reaction—the real test of the success of their efforts. Taking the project one step further, students worked on a one-on-one basis with the children, who also had been writing books. Authors consulted across age lines, sharing mutual problems of storytelling.

In my teaching experience, projects have defined learning at every grade level. Seventh graders have produced slang dictionaries, heightening knowledge and appreciation for linguistic expression. Tenth graders have written and produced soap operas, demonstrating techniques of dramatizing situations. Students exercised evaluative skills in all of these instances when they wrote peer project evaluations.

Joint curriculum design reinforces student awareness of the returns for their efforts. They not only enjoy opportunities to be creative and produce original work, but also appreciate the rewards for sustained inquiry.

Student-Generated Projects. As students and teachers become more familiar with joint curriculum design, sustained inquiry leads to student-generated projects that synthesize learning.

Interactions among students and teachers who are open to suggestion multiply learning experiences. As ideas feed off one another, novel approaches to display knowledge take shape. In social studies, eighth graders create their own colonies and negotiate treaties to establish governments that parallel a new country's beginnings. Math students graph point spreads in specific school team sports throughout a season. In biology, tenth graders debate genetic engineering and whether or not to inform a person of potential serious illnesses. Eleventh graders develop travelogues to feature cultural events and geographical distinctions of countries where certain modern languages are spoken.

Joint curriculum design assures students prominent parts in their own learning. Whether projects span a single month and represent a single unit of study, as the author exchange, slang dictionaries, or soap operas did, or whether projects synthesize a full semester, they promote original and thought-provoking work.

What projects have evolved from collaborations? What skills and talents have students exhibited? How has excellence been developed and demonstrated?

Portfolios—Selected Representations

Portfolio assessment entails a more comprehensive view of student achievement than single projects provide. An outgrowth of research on effective learning, portfolio assessment has restructured educational reform. The influential Educational Testing Service and state education departments have developed outcomes-based standards and multilevel scoring systems to recognize levels of content difficulty and demonstrated learner competence (Wiggins, 1993).

Joint curriculum design celebrates extended learning, encouraging learners to create portfolios of work samples most representative of intellectual progress.

Description. Portfolios accumulate over time. Unlike work folders, which function as catch-alls for finished and unfinished pieces, portfolios contain selective samples of student investigation, insights, and achievements. Unlike projects, which do not necessarily continue beyond certain points of understanding, portfolios represent a running record of intellectual inquiry and growth.

Portfolios may include self-, peer, and expert evaluations from teachers or outside evaluators. Rather than remain self-reports, portfolios reflect interactions with others to obtain and utilize feedback. Examples of ongoing negotiation evidence curiosity, discrimination, conviction, and resilience—intellectual strengths rarely considered in tests, but actively instrumental in lifelong learning.

To illustrate critical thinking, quality work, and identification of learning processes, portfolios offer an array of media and materials beyond paperwork or computer texts. Video and audio tapes, photographs, artifacts, and other tangible evidence attest to **personalized, interactive, integrated learning**—the principal goal of joint curriculum design.

Work Sample Selection. Work samples demonstrate exit-level competence through styles of work, mastery of skills, and student-generated inquiry. Portfolios also represent process. Partially completed pieces with attached commentaries serve to illustrate avenues of thought that learners have redirected or abandoned for specific reasons.

Learners select portfolio contents after weighing suggestions made by teachers, peers, and other interested parties. Throughout joint curriculum design, shared impressions, opinions, and visions enrich learning.

How do students demonstrate, catalog, and critique learning? What concrete evidence of growth have portfolios highlighted? How has portfolio construction changed approaches to learning and learning outcomes?

Reviews—Regrouping

Joint curriculum design involves students and teachers, as coresearchers, in regular reviews of coursework to examine influences, practices, and results.

Whereas projects tend to last for specific durations and portfolios encompass months or years of selected work, reviews supply yet another aspect of assessment. Reviews may occur on a formal or informal basis, regularly or randomly. Reviews cause individuals to court reactions and reviewers to exercise constructive, critical thinking. Reviews assist learners in extending self-reflection, weighing feedback, and regrouping. This regrouping of energies, ideas, and connections rekindles and renews further interest in learning.

Benefits.   Joint curriculum design offers learners strong intellectual, affective, and social benefits from undergoing review processes.

As Dewey (1899) described a century ago, a learner benefits from (a) criticism, question, and suggestion to raise consciousness of what has been done and what needs to be done; (b) social instincts of conversation and communication about learning; (c) constructive impulses that create tangible outlets; and (d) creative instincts that require discipline, technology, history, and design. Dewey also asserted that experiential learning promoted powers of observation, inference, reflection, and articulation of ideas.

Joint curriculum design embodies and attests to all of these benefits of critical thinking, which also characterize high quality work. Learning is enhanced and retained as a result.

Public Exhibitions.   Joint curriculum design changes the usual paper reports written for an audience of one, an evaluating teacher, into a public exchange. Joint curriculum design does not limit reviews to in-house evaluators, but encourages learners to seek outside expert advice and judgment. Students enter contests, participate in internships, or produce schoolwide or community performances.

As joint curriculum design emphasizes, students and teachers benefit from interactive learning. Whether formative or summative, reviews regard or rate work in relation to intellectual gains and anticipated ends. Public exhibitions create a forum for proliferation of information and exercise of evaluation skills. Public presentations increase work quality, not only out of an individual's sense of personal pride, but also out of appreciation for authenticity of learning experiences, no longer isolated but meant to be shared.

In collaborative ventures, colleagues and I have searched out outlets through professional organizations, corporations, and institutions of higher learning. Students have submitted work that won them recognition and rewards—free summer college courses for writing original stories, computers for writing original programs, full college scholarships. As valuable as prizes may be, the recognition from outside experts acknowledges learner competitiveness and success on a more global scale.

ALTERNATIVE OUTCOMES

Rewards of joint curriculum design extend well beyond schooling. Deliberate and dedicated interrogation of curriculum components results in multilevel learning. Collaborative and critical thinking elevate sense making through self-expression, problem-solving, discovery, and consensus building. Students and teachers construct knowledge, develop reflectiveness, raise social awareness—essentials for thoughtful and democratic living.

Constructed Knowledge

Joint curriculum design activates, nourishes, and sustains learner ability to construct meaning. Unlike traditional instruction, which transmits prescribed concepts and interpretations, joint curriculum design emphasizes learner participation in filtering information and internalizing knowledge.

Educational reformers have protested systemic routines that prevent active learning. Brown (1991) expressed frustration with unthinking curriculum:

> Ironically, the primary conditions for thoughtfulness—mystery, uncertainty, disagreement, important questions, ambiguity, curiosity—exist in every classroom. You see them in the faces of the children; you hear them in the halls. Potential learning opportunities are everywhere, but these fertile conditions are either ignored or perceived as barriers to teaching, as threats to order. (p. 234)

Consequently, Brown urged educators to become better learners themselves and to be more attuned to students, initiating change through thoughtfulness and analysis of underlying assumptions. Joint curriculum design applies the same premises to students. Insights about course content occur through active questioning of information, not passive acceptance.

With genuine development of learner voice in all areas of curriculum, joint curriculum design combines critical literacy and critical pedagogy to examine topics, ideas, and presentations. In the process, learners develop discriminating abilities to assess validity and reliability of sources, assertions, and evidence.

In what ways do students demonstrate active and individual construction of knowledge? How are they urged to delve deeper into assumptions and beliefs?

Reflectiveness—Insights

Authentic assessment fosters reflective practice by students and teachers. No longer limited to test score indicators of ability or measures of learning, students and teachers appreciate process and progress. Students shed labels and strive to live up to higher expectations (see chapter 3). Teachers reconsider goals, actions, and room for improvement. Joint curriculum design grounds beliefs in actual experiences.

After a full semester of joint curriculum design, Lorraine not only reflected on changes in her role in learning, but also recognized difficulties students encountered. She wrote:

> Teachers really are just implementers. We're really not teaching them, they're learning themselves.

> It's amazing what they can do, that I always assumed they couldn't do ... 10th grade is resisting more than the 9's ... the more they're in the old system, the harder it is for them to change.

Lorraine found the advantages of joint curriculum design out-weighed difficulties. She decided to provide extra support where needed to increase student interest and participation in the learning process:

> I feel I learned a new approach which I can implement in my daily teaching with any class. This method not only includes student involvement, it is *centered* around student involvement and response. I saw students who hadn't succeeded in my class become actively involved and move from failing to passing levels. This is an exciting adventure—because I'm not the only one in the classroom who is excited!

Lorraine and Sarah's students commented:

> I appreciate that someone is asking us how we like to learn ... if we are uncomfortable with how we are learning, then we won't learn.

> Learning how to learn and working with others are advantages for students.

We have a say in what classwork we do. We work out problems and questions.

My grades have gone up.

Ongoing assessment, integral to the success of joint curriculum design, caused students and teachers to articulate new insights and beliefs about learning. Depth of study replaced breadth. Collaboration created supportive exchange. Personal responsibility, accountability, and interest in learning escalated.

Has overall assessment of students' abilities changed? What support mechanisms facilitated student adaptation to change? Have students' beliefs in themselves as learners undergone change?

Social Awareness—Raised Consciousness

Personal backgrounds and cultural lenses frame learning. Individual life experiences, personalities, abilities, and learning styles cause learners to process information differently. Cultural conditions dictate access to knowledge (Banks, 1994; Bernstein, 1990; Freire, 1973; Giroux, 1992). Without benefit of content interrogation and social interactions, learners believe others think the same as they do.

Joint curriculum design raises consciousness and social awareness through open and honest dialogue. Differences are aired and honored in a spirit of collaboration. Students and teachers relate on a more intense level that requires attention to words, gestures, inferences, and expression.

Social dimensions of learning are integral to the quality and depth of investigation. Vygotsky (1978) recognized the power of social processes that impact learning through biases and mores underlying social interactions. Bernstein (1990), Gilligan (1982), Belenky, Clinchy, Goldberger, and Tarule (1986), and Hooks (1994) considered effects of class, gender, and race in the construction of knowledge. Greene (1995) advocated empathy in the search for meaning—awareness of privilege by the privileged, sensitivity toward the marginalized, and imaginative agency for social change in order to support richer lives across socioeconomic lines.

Joint curriculum design alerts teachers and students to these vital issues and transformative aspects of the learning process. Authentic exchanges and alternative, ongoing assessment gives voice to all learners, enabling them to challenge information, exchange ideas, and demonstrate intellectual acuity.

Joint curriculum design celebrates life-giving capacities of constructing knowledge, reflecting on consequences, and effecting social consciousness.

SUMMARY

This chapter delineated the purposes, forms, processes, and signs of progress that joint curriculum design measures through ongoing, authentic assessments. Examples suggest how to engage students in demonstrating skills and knowledge on a regular basis and organizing presentations as culminating activities shared with audiences.

Behind-the-Scenes Mental Preparation

1. As you consider the scope of joint curriculum design, list assessment methods you generally apply to ascertain student progress. Apply three adjectives to characterize each item on the list. Review the terms. If similar words keep reappearing, what alternative assessments might be needed to provide different feedback of student learning?

2. Outline a plan for developing portfolio assessment. Include procedures for designing different tasks, recording tangible and intangible growth, reviewing contents with students on individual and group bases, and confirming gists of conferencing.

3. Identify changes in teaching that have occurred as a result of authentic assessments. How do you approach a new unit? How much collaboration are students permitted from the start? When do you find it necessary to take charge? How do you check for student understanding? When do you administer tests?

On-Stage Tryouts

1. Discuss tests and measurements with students. Elicit reasons for varying assessments and analyze student satisfaction with current evaluation procedures. Even if students seem comfortable with

the status quo, broach alternatives and outline the additional information they produce. Select a new measure for experimentation.

2. Propose a project for which students will generate some or all criteria for areas of investigation, timeframes, and tangible products. The length of the project will depend on the breadth of the topic and student interest. Schedule interim reports and debriefings to assure students of support and decide how learning will be demonstrated to the class as a whole. Set aside time for peer and project evaluation.

10

On Tour:
Future Applications

୫ ◆ ଓ

Successful troupes and productions go on tour; active participation
in joint curriculum design prompts students and teachers to design
future applications.

Theatrical successes take on a life of their own. Repertory theaters
form, individual actors sign contracts for new roles, stage productions are replicated across the country and world. Enriched understandings of performance strengths and production content extend
to new collaborative endeavors.

Joint curriculum design expands curriculum planning and implementation in similar fashion. Teachers who create a climate
conducive to collaboration with students discover renewed interest
in working more directly and reciprocally with others to increase
effective learning. Students develop voice, resources, and responsibility for learning that they are eager to sustain. The excitement of
learning that results when all above considerations coalesce is
self-perpetuating. Integral learning and familiarity with more strategies for learning lead to testing the potential for future applications.

**What new approaches to learning will teachers try? How will
students become more active in future classes? What questions have not yet been answered?**

APPROACHES TO LEARNING

Considering the magnitude of problems plaguing public education,
approaches to learning have undergone only minor changes

throughout the 20th century. Despite efforts like the Eight-Year Study (Aikin, 1942) and student-centered learning (Hemming, 1948; Schaefer, 1967), public schools have been entrenched in traditional teaching. Efforts to reconceptualize teaching in order to improve learning persistently materialize.

The 1970s burst into restructuring secondary school curriculum to counter the inadequacy of course offerings (Unruh & Alexander 1970) and the plight of teachers within inflexible systems (Lortie, 1975). Advocates suggested greater learner choice through independent study, unstructured learning, open classrooms, mini-courses, and team teaching (Glatthorn, 1975). Critics claimed wide experimentation watered down course content, reduced individual responsibility, and eliminated rigor.

The 1980s reverted to back-to-basics curriculum and top-down mandates for the first few years, then made an about-face and focused on teacher empowerment to change school systems from the bottom up (Lather, 1986; Maeroff, 1988; Schon, 1987). Review of coursework led to greater integration of topics and skills within specific disciplines (Brandt, 1988) and inclusion of contributions by members of marginalized populations (Cummins, 1989). To accommodate these changes, teacher preparation faced new demands (Goodlad, 1991; Lieberman, 1990).

The 1990s centered on learning experiences and learner differences. Research findings challenged school systems, personnel, and content. Cooperative learning, gender-fair education, and diversity predominated in professional literature and conferences (Banks, 1994; Lampert, 1991; Sadker & Sadker, 1994). Societal changes, inclusion, information explosion, and technological advances forced school districts to develop strategic plans for improvement, reaching out to communities, corporations, and institutions of higher learning to create partnerships. Interdisciplinary learning and block scheduling began to materialize.

Entering the 21st century, educational reformers strive to exert more influence. With projections indicating that secondary school students will change career paths on an average of seven times during their working years, they urge school districts to prepare students for critical thinking, problem solving, cooperative learning, and joint decision making.

Joint curriculum design embraces these issues and offers powerful solutions through collaboration between students and teachers.

Education is not done to anyone—as learners, students, and teachers choose goals, methods, and content. They interact with resources and network with others to investigate topics and derive understandings. They devise plans, implement ideas, and assess progress. The comprehensiveness and thoroughness behind joint curriculum design facilitates active participation and mutual ownership.

Teachers

Teachers approach learning differently after becoming acquainted with the premises and implementation of joint curriculum design. They give students center stage. They spotlight each learner's try-outs in pursuit of knowledge and act as prompters behind the scenes.

Indispensable to the learning process, teachers engage students individually and exchange ideas to interrogate coursework, rather than dictate assignments and administer examinations. They encourage exploration and experimentation. Classroom environments invite all learners to research, interact, and draw tentative conclusions. Teachers join in discovery learning and provide unique perspectives.

As a consequence of joint curriculum design, veteran and prospective teachers have grown professionally, presenting workshops at state conferences, explaining experiences and rewards of collaboration with students. They network and promote interactive learning among colleagues and students. Many student teachers have demonstrated joint curriculum design to cooperating teachers who adapt learning situations accordingly.

Joint curriculum design enlivens every meeting of teachers and students. Teachers cultivate curiosity through choice and flexibility through trust, modeling for students necessary attitudes toward inquiry and research.

Students

Joint curriculum design empowers students. No longer passively facing a teacher who stands in the front of the room, students actively participate in studying course content and interact with one another to discover ideas, link concepts, pose and solve problems.

Students practice metacognition, determining how they learn best and what other options exist to be tried. They exercise skills of discrimination and evaluation as they process information. They activate imagination, creating original ideas and bringing them to fruition. Students develop social skills, working in conjunction with teachers, peers, and other resources to achieve common goals.

Joint curriculum design invigorates all learners, signalling them to take on personal responsibility and accountability for learning. Students respond well to this challenge. They not only utilize the opportunity to make learning more meaningful in the present, but also realize they have the right to take the initiative to interrogate information and negotiate learning throughout school—lessons to carry throughout life.

Strategies

Experimentation with joint curriculum design rejuvenates teachers, empowers students, and strengthens the bonds between them. As coresearchers, students and teachers appreciate action research, critical literacy, and critical pedagogy. They collaborate and reflect on goals, methods, and actions; they search out resources, interrogate information, communicate insights and concerns, share feedback, change direction, and assess progress.

Learning logs, working folders, and dialectic journals document ideas, trials, and errors—informing students and teachers of strategies that proved effective and strategies that require adjustments. Joint efforts to improve learning fortify teachers, students, and curriculum content.

Joint curriculum design expands through geometric progressions. Each teacher and student multiplies possibilities. Each new unit of study or class adds permutations. Collaborative, interactive learning of students and teachers continues to inspire new strategies.

What innovations have begun to form? What new adaptations or alterations of strategies have arisen? How will you involve students in future applications?

Joint curriculum design respects students and teachers as agents of rigorous learning and constructive change. Differentiation, investigation, independence, and individualization influence active participation. Joint ownership in curriculum design nurtures empathetic, creative, critical thinkers, provides access to knowledge to all learners, enlivens education, sharpens minds, and elevates spirits. Future applications await auditions.

References

8O ◆ C8

Aikin, W. M. (1942). *Adventure in American education: Vol. 1. The story of the Eight-Year Study.* New York: Harper & Brothers.

Apple, M. (1990). *Ideology and curriculum* (2nd ed.). New York: Routledge.

Ayers, W. (1991). Grounded insights. In K. Jervis & C. Montag (Eds.), *Progressive education for the 1990's* (pp. 125–133). New York: Teachers College Press.

Banks, J. (1994). *Multiethnic education* (3rd ed.). Boston: Allyn & Bacon.

Barell, J. (1991). *Teaching for thoughtfulness.* New York: Longman.

Barker, R. G. (1968). *Ecological psychology.* Stanford, CA: Stanford University Press.

Barth, R. S. (1972). *Open education and the American school.* New York: Agathon Press.

Bateman, W. L. (1990). *Open to question.* San Francisco: Jossey-Bass.

Belenky, M., Clinchy, B., Goldberger, N., & Tarule, J. (1986). *Women's ways of knowing.* New York: Basic Books.

Bernstein, B. (1975). *Class, codes, and control* (Vol. 3). London: Routledge & Kegan Paul.

Bernstein, B. (1990). *The structuring of pedagogic discourse: Vol. 4. Class, codes, and control.* London: Routledge.

Brandt, R. S. (1988). *The content of the curriculum* (ASCD Yearbook). Garboe Printing Co.

Bremer, A., & Bremer, J. (1972). *Open education.* New York: Holt, Rinehart & Winston.

Britzman, D. (1991). *Practice makes practice.* Albany: State University of New York Press.

Brown, R. G. (1991). *Schools of thought.* San Francisco: Jossey-Bass.

Bruner, J. (1966). *Toward a theory of instruction.* Cambridge, MA: Belknap Press.

Burns, R. B., & Anderson, L. W. (1987). The activity structure of lesson segments. *Curriculum Inquiry, 17,* 31–53.

Butler, K. (1984). *Learning and teaching style: In theory and practice.* Columbia, CT: The Learner's Dimension.

Carini, P. (1991). Honoring diversity/striving for inclusion. In K. Jervis & C. Montag (Eds.), *Progressive education for the 1990's* (pp. 17–31). New York: Teachers College Press.

Cazden, C. B. (1988). *Classroom discourse.* Portsmouth, NH: Heineman.

Chenitz, W. C., & Swanson, J. M. (1986). *From practice to grounded theory.* Menlo Park, CA: Addison-Wesley.

Cook, A. (1991). The high school inquiry classroom. In Jervis & Montag (Eds.), *Progressive education for the 1990's* (pp. 149–151). New York: Teachers College Press.

Cox, D. W. (1972). *The city as a schoolhouse: The story of the Parkway Program.* Valley Forge, PA: Judson Press.

Cuban, L. (1990). Reforming again, again, and again. *Educational Researcher, 19,* 3–13.

Cummins, J. (1989). Empowering minority students: A framework for intervention. In *Empowering teachers and students* (pp. 1–18). Cambridge, MA: Harvard Educational Review.

Delpit, L. D. (1989). The silenced dialogue: Power and pedagogy in educating other people's children. In *Empowering teachers and students* (pp. 78–95). Cambridge, MA: Harvard Educational Review.

Dewey, J. (1899). *The school and society.* Chicago: University of Chicago Press.

Dewey, J. (1948). *Experience and education.* New York: Macmillan.

Doyle, W. (1977). Learning the classroom environment. *Journal of Teacher Education,* XXVIII, 51–55.

Egan, K. (1990). *Romantic understanding.* New York: Routledge.

Engstrom, D. (1993, April). *Feedback.* Paper presented at the Cooperating Teacher Workshop, Ursinus College, Collegeville, PA.

Ferdman, B. M. (1990). Literacy and cultural identity. *Harvard Educational Review, 60,* 181–204.

Fraser, B. (Ed.). (1986). *The study of learning environments.* Salem, OR: Assessment Research.

Freedman, J. L. (1975). *Crowding and behavior.* San Francisco: Freeman.

Freire, P. (1973). *The pedagogy of the oppressed.* New York: Seabury Press.

Freire, P. (1991, April). *The politics, power, and education in Sao Paulo, Brazil.* Paper presented at the meeting of the American Education Research Association, Chicago.

Gardner, H. (1991). *The unschooled mind.* New York: Basic Books.

Gardner, H. (1995). Reflections on multiple intelligences: Myths and messages. *Phi Delta Kappan,* 77, 200–209.

Gifford, R. (1987). *Environmental psychology.* Newton, MA: Allyn & Bacon.

Giles, H. H., McCuthan, S. P., & Zechiel, A. N. (1942). *Adventure in American education: Vol. 2. Exploring the curriculum.* New York: Harper & Brothers.

Gilligan, C. (1982). *In a different voice.* Cambridge, MA: Harvard University Press.

Giroux, H. (1988). *Teachers as intellectuals.* Granby, MA: Bergin & Garvey.

Giroux, H. (1992). *Border crossings.* New York: Routledge.

Giroux, H. (1994). Doing cultural studies: Youth and the challenge of pedagogy. *Harvard Educational Review, 64,* 278–308.

Glaser, R. (1990, April). *The maturing of the relationship between the science of learning and cognition and educational practice.* Paper presented at the meeting of the American Education Research Association, Boston.

Glasser, W. (1986). *Control theory in the classroom.* New York: Harper & Row.

Glatthorn, A. A. (1975). *Alternatives in education: Schools and programs.* New York: Dodd Mead.

Goodlad, J. (1991). *Teachers for our nation's schools.* San Francisco: Jossey-Bass.

Grannis, J. C. (1980). Classroom culture and the problem of control. In F. W. Forshay (Ed.), *Considered action for curriculum improvement* (ASCD Yearbook, pp. 43–69). Alexandria, VA: ASCD.

Greene, M. (1971). Curriculum and consciousness. *Teachers College Record*, 73, 253–269.

Greene, M. (1978). *Landscapes of learning*. New York: Teachers College Press.

Greene, M. (1988). *The dialectic of freedom*. New York: Teachers College Press.

Greene, M. (1995). *Releasing the imagination*. San Francisco: Jossey-Bass.

Gregorc, A. F. (1984). *Style delineator*. Columbia, CT: The Learner's Dimension.

Gross, P. A. (1991, December). *Interactive reading in the secondary level*. Paper presented at the National Reading Conference, Palm Springs, CA. (ERIC Document Reproduction Service No. ED 359 490)

Gross, P. A. (1992a). *Actions and perceptions of students and teachers when changing toward a whole language instructional mode in secondary level English classrooms*. Unpublished doctoral dissertation, Teachers College, Columbia University, New York.

Gross, P. A. (1992b, December). *Shared meaning: Whole language reader response at the secondary level*. Paper presented at the National Reading Conference, San Antonio, TX. (ERIC Document Reproduction Service No. ED 359 491)

Gross, P. A. (1996). Grounding theory into practice. *Teaching Education, 88*(1), 37–44.

Grumet, M. R. (1988). *Bitter milk*. Amherst: University of Massachusetts Press.

Hall, E. T. (1966). *The hidden dimension*. New York: Doubleday.

Hemming, J. (1948). *Teach them to live*. London: Longmans, Green & Co.

Heyman, M. (1978). *Places and spaces: Environmental psychology in education*. Bloomington, IN: PDK Educational Foundation.

hooks, b. (1994). *Teaching to transgress*. New York: Routledge.

Ittelson, W. H. (Ed.). (1973). *Environment and cognition*. New York: Seminar Press.

Johnson, D. W., & Johnson, R. T. (1991). *Learning together and alone* (3rd ed). Englewood Cliffs, NJ: Prentice-Hall.

Johnson, D. W., Johnson, R. T., Holubec, E. J., & Roy, P. (1984). *Circles of learning: Cooperation in the classroom*. Alexandria, VA: Association of Supervision and Curriculum Development.

Joyce, B., & Weil, M. (1995). *Models of teaching* (5th ed.). Boston: Allyn & Bacon.

Kagan, S. (1988). *Cooperative learning: Resources for teachers*. Riverside: University of California Press.

Keefe, J. W. (1989). Personalized education. In H. J. Walberg & J. J. Lane (Eds.), *Organizing for learning: Toward the 21st century* (pp. 72–81). Reston, VA: National Association of Secondary School Principals.

Kilpatrick, W. H. (1925). *Foundations of methods*. New York: Macmillan.

Koneya, M. (1976). Location and interaction in row and column seating arrangements. *Environment and Behavior, 8*, 265–282.

Kozol, J. (1991). *Savage inequalities*. New York: Crown.

Lampert, M. (1991, April). *Representing practice: Learning and teaching about teaching and learning*. Paper presented at the meeting of the American Education Research Association, Chicago.

Lather, P. (1986). Research as praxis. *Harvard Educational Review, 56*, 257–277.

Lieberman, A. (1990). *Schools as collaborative cultures: Creating the future now*. New York: The Falmer Press.

Lortie, D. (1975). *Schoolteacher.* Chicago: University of Chicago Press.

Loughlin, C. E., & Suina, J. H. (1982). *The learning environment.* New York: Teachers College Press.

Maeroff, G. I. (1988). *The empowerment of teachers.* New York: Teachers College Press.

Martinello, M. L., & Cook, G. E. (1994). *Interdisciplinary inquiry in teaching and learning.* New York: Merrill.

McLaren, P. (1995). *Critical pedagogy and predatory culture.* London: Routledge.

Mehlinger, H.D. (1996). School reform in the information age. *Phi Delta Kappan, 77,* 400–407.

Meier, D. (1995a). How our schools could be. *Phi Delta Kappan, 76,* 369–373.

Meier, D. (1995b). *The power of their ideas.* Boston: Beacon Press.

Merriam, S. B. (1990). *Case study research in education.* San Francisco: Jossey-Bass.

Nieto, S. (1996). *Affirming diversity* (2nd ed.). New York: Longman.

Noddings, N. (1984). *Caring: A feminine approach to ethics and moral education.* Berkeley: University of California Press.

Noddings, N. (1990, April). *Theoretical and practical concerns about small groups.* Paper presented at the meeting of the American Education Research Association, Boston.

Noddings, N. (1995). A morally defensible mission for schools in the 21st century. *Phi Delta Kappan, 76,* 365–368.

O'Neil, J. (1995). On technology and schools. *Educational Leadership, 53,* 6–12.

Orenstein, P. (1994). *School girls.* New York: Doubleday.

Ornstein, A. C., & Hunkins, F. P. (1988). *Curriculum: Foundations, principles, and issues.* Englewood Cliffs, NJ: Prentice-Hall.

Perrone, V. (1991). Large purposes. In K. Jervis & C. Montag (Eds.), *Progressive education for the 1990's* (pp. 9–16). New York: Teachers College Press.

Reagan, S. B., Fox, T., & Bleich, D. (Eds.). (1994). *Writing with.* Albany: State University of New York Press.

Rosenshine, B., & Stevens, R. (1986). Teaching functions. In M. Wittrock (Ed.), *Handbook of research on teaching* (3rd ed., pp. 376–391). New York: Macmillan.

Sadker, M., & Sadker, D. (1994). *Failing at fairness.* New York: Scribner's.

Sarason, S. B. (1993). *The case for change.* San Francisco: Jossey-Bass.

Schaefer, R. (1967). *School as a center of inquiry.* (John Dewey Society Lecture No. 9). New York: Harper & Row.

Schon, D. A. (1987). *Educating the reflective practitioner.* San Francisco: Jossey-Bass.

Schon, D. A. (1990, November). *The theory of inquiry: Dewey's legacy to education.* Speech delivered at Teachers College, Columbia University, New York.

Sergiovanni, T. J. (1994). *Building community in schools.* San Francisco: Jossey-Bass.

Sizer, T. R. (1985). *Horace's compromise.* Boston: Houghton Mifflin.

Slavin, R. E., Sharon, S., Kagan, S., Hertz-Lazarowitz, R., Webb, C., & Schmuck, R. (Eds.). (1985). *Learning to cooperate, cooperating to learn.* New York: Plenum Press.

Smiley, S. (1987). *Theatre: The human art.* New York: Harper & Row.

Sternberg, R. J. (1990). *Metaphors of mind.* New York: Cambridge University Press.

Strauss, A. L. (1990). *Qualitative analysis for social scientists.* Cambridge, UK: Cambridge University Press.

Totten, C. F. (1985, April). *Participants in learning, not spectators.* Paper presented at the University System of Georgia Statewide Conference on Developmental Studies, Jerkyll Island, GA.

Unruh, G., & Alexander, W.H. (1970). *Innovations in secondary education.* New York: Holt, Rinehart & Winston.

Vygotsky, L. S. (1978). *Mind in society—The development of higher psychological processes.* Cambridge, MA: Harvard University Press.

Walberg, H. J. (1990). Productive teaching and instruction: Assessing the knowledge base. *Phi Delta Kappan, 71,* 470–478.

Walberg, H. J., & Lane, J. J. (Eds.). (1989). *Organizing for learning: Toward the 21st century.* Reston, VA: NASSP.

Wasley, P. A. (1991). *Teachers who lead.* New York: Teachers College Press.

Wiggins, G. (1993). *Assessing student performance.* San Francisco: Jossey-Bass.

Wigginton, E. (1985). *Sometimes a shining moment: The Foxfire experience.* New York: Anchor.

Author Index

Subject Index